BADASS IT SUPPORT

BADASS IT SUPPORT

BEN BRENNAN

LIONCREST
PUBLISHING

BADASS IT SUPPORT

ISBN   978-1-5445-1027-9 *Paperback*
       978-1-5445-1028-6 *Ebook*

This book is dedicated to Monster, Quasi, and Rebbe, the three loves of my life. I'm a happier man every single day that I wake up to see your faces.

CONTENTS

INTRODUCTION

I recently became the director of IT for Oath, which Verizon formed when it combined AOL and Yahoo!, my former employer. Oath has about twelve thousand employees and reaches about 1.3 billion users monthly. Before this massive merger, we ran a 24/7 IT shop at Yahoo! supporting employees around the globe on five continents. And we were fucking good at it. During my tenure at Yahoo!, we threw out the IT department's twenty-year-old playbook and dated metrics, and in the course of two years, we took our customer satisfaction scores from DMV to Ritz Carlton levels, with about a third of the staff we started with. We transformed the team culture and rallied everyone behind the mission of Badass IT Support. Now, as the IT director at Oath, my new team and I are going back to square one and are on track to do the same thing all over again with this exciting new company.

But things didn't start like that...

A lot of people I work with now think I'm hot shit and that I've always been a Badass IT Support guru. This is categorically untrue. To quote AC/DC, it's a long way to the top if you wanna rock 'n roll. When I got my first job as an IT consultant, I had to Google the word "consultant" because I wasn't sure what one was. I was *that* naïve.

As it turns out, I was naïve about a lot of things concerning IT. For example, I thought it was all about providing a kickass customer experience, the way I'd provided five-star service in some of my previous IT jobs or when I was a waiter or bartender. When I worked those jobs, my livelihood depended on *serving* people. It depended on anticipating their needs and exceeding their expectations. If I didn't do that, I made shitty tips. If I made shitty tips, I couldn't pay my rent. I never had that problem because I provided mind-blowing service, every time.

That first consulting job was with a company called Box, a cloud-based content management and file-sharing service. I'd met one of the founders, Sam Ghods, in my neighborhood bar in the Mission District of San Francisco. He and Box's CIO, Ben Haines, had been impressed with the IT work I had done in my previous jobs with Jawbone, Twitter, and Hack Reactor, and Box needed some help in that area.

Working at Box was a revelation for me. At my previous gigs, we had built teams from scratch made up of scrappy, fun artists who had a blast at work and were all indoctrinated into my naïve vision that IT support should be customer-centric and a badass experience for our customers. At Box, I would not build my own IT team but inherit an already-established one. This is when I learned that not everyone shared my ideas about how IT support should be. I thought it was a no-brainer that IT should be focused on providing badass service for a company's employees, who are, in a sense, your customers. I thought IT was about cranking up some music, putting art on the walls, and having a party space where people could come have a blast while we fixed their shit for them. Turns out this was not the universal experience for most companies when coming to IT for help. In fact, it was pretty far from it.

I FACED A BIG CHALLENGE

The IT crew at Box was a fun group of guys, for sure. I love them to this day, but let's be honest, the department needed a little work. I remember showing up on my first day to a dirty desk with random Post-it notes and sticky coffee mugs all over the surface. But when I got back from orientation, someone had cleaned it up and polished it for me. It glistened. This hipster guy named Dom from the IT team came up to me and said, "Hey, man. I know it's your first day, and I just wanted you to have a nice desk."

Cool, right? I thought this was a very good sign. Customer service at its best! I thanked him, and he went back to click-clacking the keys on his fancy gamer keyboard with his two-hundred-dollar hipster headphones on. Off to a great start, right?

Then the customers, our employees, began entering the office. At one point, an engineer came in with his computer. He was not a confident English speaker, so he shyly approached Dom and told him in halting phrases that there was something wrong with his laptop. After a couple of beats, Dom pulled down a headphone from one ear.

"Go fuck yourself," he told the engineer. Then he pulled his headphones back up and resumed typing. The rest of the IT team sitting around us burst out laughing. I died a little—okay, a lot—inside. I would definitely be earning my consulting fee for this gig.

The engineer stood there for a moment taken aback by Dom's dismissal, and then turned and walked away, cradling his disabled laptop. You could see his shoulders sag as he stared at his blank screen.

Suddenly Dom pulled off his headphones, laughed, and called the guy back over. "I'm just fucking with you, man. What's your problem?" and proceeded to fix the guy's issue in a matter of minutes.

I was stunned. Dom was trying to be funny, I guess, but there was no way he could ever erase how he made that engineer feel. If nothing else, Dom showed a lack of empathy, to say the least. If Dom made comments like that to this engineer, what did he say to other customers? Once you've given someone the impression you don't want to talk to them, no amount of reassurance will rebuild that relationship. Trust me on this. Before I got into IT, I earned a master's degree in psychology and worked as a psychotherapist for two years. People remember shit like that.

Dom had embedded a cruel little piece of shrapnel under the engineer's skin, and there is no way to remove that without leaving a scar.

This was my first inkling that I had my work cut out for me. Over time, Dom turned out to be one of the nicest guys you'll meet. He is great to hang out with at a bar, and he would do anything for a friend. He's one of my favorite people to this day. But his attitude at work toward that one engineer, I learned, prevailed in the IT departments that I would work with over the next several years. As a new consultant, my first order of business became clear: we need to ramp up our game.

IT departments at even some of the largest and best companies in the world today are entrenched in outmoded processes and attitudes like this. They follow decades-old procedures that are outdated and process-heavy, and their workers are allowed to treat customers like they are a distraction instead of the whole reason our jobs exist.

Ask most people you meet how they feel about the IT department at their company, and you'll hear a groan and see them put on the stink face. IT workers are dismissive and grumpy. When a customer comes to them with a problem, their answer is to sigh loudly and often (still!) tell them to turn their computer off and on again to see if that fixes the problem. It's literally their job to fix employees' computers, but when you ask them to do that, they grunt and act like you interrupted them. They act like you pulled them away from more important work, even though the primary purpose of their job is to help you, their customer and coworker, be as productive as possible at your job.

We have some work to do, people.

WHAT YOU'LL GET FROM THIS BOOK

This book will tell you how your company can have a Badass IT Support team that blows the minds of the customers you support. Other companies have done it; why not yours?

If you don't buy in to the fact that there is a problem—if

you think IT is awesome as it is and doesn't need improving, if you're stoked on the status quo and it meets your personal standards of excellence as it is—then this book is not for you. But if you suspect your customers aren't so enthusiastic about the IT support they're receiving, maybe you should read on.

The fact that you bought a book called *Badass IT Support* with a leather-clad biker on the cover tells me you might appreciate a different spin on what IT support can and should be. If so, hop on, and let's go for a ride. I've been down this road more than a few times, and this book is my chance to share the roadmap with more people than I could help individually as a consultant. This is how you fix the system. This is how you go from a lose-lose to a win-win. Everyone relax—this is gonna be awesome.

WHAT I'VE LEARNED

During nearly ten years as an IT manager and consultant at start-ups like Twitter and long-standing companies like Yahoo!, I saw the value of changing the culture of IT departments. I helped transform them from dark, remote, and unfriendly dens of unkempt neckbeards to bright, cheerful, and inspiring departments that play a powerful role in improving a company's bottom line and ramping up employee productivity to light speed.

While many CEOs think of IT as a "necessary evil"—an uber-expensive service they hate but feel like they must provide—I have developed an approach that makes IT a significant contributor to a company's success. My approach turns surly, underwhelming operations into nimble, delightful departments that customers love and executives intuitively see the value in.

IT leaders who follow the prescriptions in this book will find their departments treated with more respect by management. They'll learn how to connect better with their customers, and they'll find that focusing on what those customers need and want makes their own IT workers happier and more satisfied. It's a win-win-win. IT managers will see their own careers take off, and they'll get to see their entry-level techs move into higher-paying dream jobs in other departments like marketing and engineering. I've seen this happen over and over again, and it's my favorite part of the job. Like I said, everyone wins. How can you argue with that?

If you're a CEO, this book will help you form a vision for your company. I'll introduce you to a new approach I've honed over the last decade that leads to killer customer service. This new approach offers continual improvement by measuring meaningful new metrics never before used by old-fashioned IT departments. The best part is that your IT strategy will write itself because it's based directly on your customers' feedback.

If you're an IT worker, I can show you why you need to drop the old shtick and adopt a new persona, one closer to the real you, rather than the "IT version." This book will show you how to get better at your job and set yourself up for higher-paying gigs in the future. Don't worry: I'm not telling you to wear a necktie and pleated Dockers. I will suggest you smile more, learn better interpersonal communication, and work harder to earn your customer's trust. Believe me, it will pay off for you. You will look forward to going to work every day.

Regardless of the size of your company, this book will show IT managers how to inspire and transform their IT departments into customer-centric, world-class orgs. You'll learn a practical, proven method for listening to your customers and adjusting to their changing needs. You'll come to understand the concrete value of not just servicing your customers but blowing their socks off with world-class customer support.

That ideal is what I call Badass IT Support. It's easier to achieve than you might think.

WHAT THE HELL DO I KNOW? THE BACKSTORY

Being an IT director at Oath is a long way from where I started, to say the least. After graduating from Texas A&M and then getting my master's degree, I worked for two years as a licensed therapist in Texas. I've always enjoyed helping people, but the work didn't feel right for me. It didn't help that I was managing a department of twelve people and only making around $40,000 a year.

I've always had a powerful artistic streak, so in 2008, I dropped out of the working world and spent a year traveling in Guatemala and other parts of Central America, playing music and writing. I fell upon the idea of writing a book about my life, so after a year in Central America, I moved to Berkeley to work on it.

I was dirt poor and living in a co-op. I would write five or six hours a day, and it would be awesome. Then the next day I would look at what I wrote, and it wouldn't seem so awesome. I'm not a bad writer, but I struggled to create something I was proud of and never tried to get the book published. Occasionally, I'd decide I needed to get a job at Starbucks, and I would download the application. The browser I used would number the PDF every time I downloaded the application. I was on version nine before I decided I was never going to apply. I needed a new plan.

To top it off, I was dating this rich girl who was a creative director at a major search engine. She made high six figures, and I made around $400 a month. I couldn't even afford the four bucks to take the train into San Francisco. Even my own mother teased me about my situation; she said if I didn't get paid to write, then all I was doing every day was journaling.

The writer's life was *not* working out.

WAX ON, WAX OFF: MY BIG BREAK

I'd stayed in touch with a friend of mine from high school back in Texas, and about this time we both happened to be living in the Bay Area. But while I was a starving writer, he was making it big working for tech companies running their IT departments. He was introducing me to people he knew in advertising and the creative world, trying to help me get a job with them, when one day, he said, "Fuck it. Why don't you just get into IT?" I didn't know what to think at first; even though I knew how to fix Macs, I had no formal training in IT. He was the kind of dude who didn't give a shit, so he "overstated" my qualifications a bit and helped me land a job at Pivotal Labs, a software and services company in the Bay Area.

I had to learn everything from scratch. I kept a list during the day of everything I needed to fix, and at night I'd go home and Google the problems and learn how to solve them. When someone asked for my help, I would look things over, take some notes, and spend all night researching the problem. The next morning, I would come in, find the person, and say, "Hey, I found your solution." This strategy was surprisingly effective. It was like working so hard to cheat on a test that you accidentally learned the material even better than if you had been studying.

My friend also helped train me with all the basic skills I'd need to be an IT professional. Remember the *Karate Kid* movies? Well, my friend was my Mr. Miyagi. I knew Macs well, but I didn't know much about Windows computers, so he put me through some informal training. He'd do things like tie a T-shirt over my eyes like a blindfold and have me upgrade the RAM on a PC just by feel.

We had a blast doing this unconventional training regimen. He made me buy a huge whiteboard from Office Depot, and every day when we got home from work, he would use it to put me through all these crazy drills.

The training went beyond technology. This was a next-level Mr. Miyagi training regime. In one drill, he described a typical day where the CEO comes up to me and says he's having a board meeting and the projectors in the board-room aren't working. Then two executive assistants stop by, and they have problems with something else. In the middle of all that, some sales staffers call, and they have a million-dollar pitch in five minutes and can't open the PowerPoint for it. So, the drill was to make a list of all the competing problems and decide in which order you will fix each one. My head was spinning, but it was certainly great preparation for working in IT.

The most important thing he taught me was confidence and logical troubleshooting. His attitude was that if you approached it the right way, you could solve any problem. Was it hardware or software? Was it a system problem or a user problem? Narrow it down and fix it. You have to face any challenge knowing there's always a solution.

When Black Friday came, I took advantage of the sales and maxed out my credit card buying PC parts and building a gaming PC so I could learn about hardware. I also got all kinds of certifications for fixing Macs. I couldn't afford the training from Apple, but I knew I had to learn all this ancient Apple stuff, like how to fix cathode ray tubes and shit like that, so I "borrowed" some training materials, studied it on my own, and got Apple certified.

My friend continued to send me on these crazy missions to learn different things, and I soaked up all this knowledge on the fly. It was like getting a free education. I also made twenty-five dollars an hour, and I was thrilled. At work, we had free catered breakfasts, catered lunches, and free expensive juices in the fridge—it was not hard to make the transition from being dirt poor and living in a co-op in Berkeley to this. Our kooky antics at work were fun for the engineers at Pivotal Labs, too, having this curly haired

IT Jesus running around the office upgrading RAM while blindfolded. This was not the kind of IT they were used to, and they loved it.

When I had developed enough IT chops, my friend hooked me up with a headhunter who landed me a job at Jawbone—the outfit that makes Bluetooth earpieces. At the time, they had thirty-five employees, but then they got a shit-ton of venture capital shortly after I arrived, and by the time I left, they had quintupled to around 250 employees. After that, Twitter, which was a customer of Pivotal Labs, gave me a call, and I went to work there. Twitter had just a few hundred employees at the time and wasn't making any money, but that changed, of course. After a few years and a historic IPO, a bunch of Twitter guys left to start a coding school called Hack Reactor. I became their IT director. Then I met Sam Ghods and went to work at Box as a consultant.

PROVING YOUR VALUE EVERY DAY

My background gives me a much different outlook on IT than most people who enter the field. I didn't learn IT the traditional way, and this has made me less respectful of antiquated standards and more grateful that we get to work at some of the world's coolest companies and make good money doing it.

I've had to hustle throughout my professional life, and

I've learned that you must prove your worth every day. Some folks in IT don't seem to share that work ethic, but that attitude is what helped me succeed. You must make yourself indispensable to your customers by being the best there is at whatever job you have. That, more than anything, is what I try to teach the IT crews I work with. Your success is measured by your customers and the value you provide to them.

A big reason IT workers don't hustle to be the best is that they have no competition. Listen, companies only have one IT department, and IT workers know it. Why should IT folks bend over backward for a customer when they know the customer has no other choice but to play by their rules? IT is not like other customer-facing industries. If you're pissed at Uber, you can switch to Lyft. If you don't like one hotel, you can move to another. That's not possible when you work at a company that has one IT department. Chapter Four of this book dives deep into how to motivate IT workers who have no competition.

My approach in response to this has been to inject some urgency into the IT workplace. Even when your IT department has a monopoly in your company, IT managers and workers must find a way to work like their jobs depend on it. IT teams must transform themselves into customer-centric, badass support departments that provide measurable value to the company, and they must do so of their own volition. My attitude is this: Let's *choose* to be awesome rather than being *told* to be awesome. Let's do it because *it's more fun that way.*

When I worked at Jawbone and Twitter, we did awesome shit all day because we had fun doing it. I was naïve, so it never occurred to me that IT departments would operate any other way. I mean, we worked for these great companies, so it seemed obvious that we should earn our money by going above and beyond expectations. If you love your work and you're grateful for the job, why would you do anything else?

Another important thing I have learned over the years and built my consulting business on is that Badass IT Support can have a direct impact on the company's bottom line. Even as a technician, I would always study the business value of IT and read everything I could on the topic, and that's how I realized that IT could do a lot more than just fix trackpads and load printer drivers. Before, I wanted to do badass IT because it was more fun than doing mediocre IT. Later, I learned there are economic reasons for delivering badass IT, and this fired me up even more. If your IT team is awesome, more people will use them, less shit will break, and employee productivity will go through the roof. That's the reasoning I've used with every IT team I've worked with. What's the point of doing this job if it isn't to blow someone's socks off? Who wouldn't want to be badass at what they do?

GETTING STARTED

None of what I tell CIOs, IT managers, and IT support workers in this book is rocket science. It *is* revolutionary, but it's something anyone working in or running an IT department can accomplish. It boils down to a very simple premise: listen to your customers, find out what they need, and then exceed their expectations.

The process is simple, but the transformation isn't always easy. When you show up and say, "Hey, let's do some badass customer support today!" some people in your IT department will roll their eyes and refuse to participate. That's fine. If they don't want to be there, find another place for them—preferably out of the way so they can't interfere. I don't take firing lightly—there's a whole chapter in this book about dealing with difficult situations like this—but you can't half-ass Badass IT Support. A mind-blowing customer experience must be everyone's highest priority if you're going to win.

Change has to come. It's time. Let's be honest: there is no way someone like me could be as successful as I am if IT had its shit together. I'm successful not in spite of the fact, but because of the fact that I'm an outsider—a frustrated writer and former psychotherapist who had a lot of things to prove and needed to earn a living. If I can find success, so can you.

Are you ready to get badass?

PART ONE

ENTERING THE WORLD OF IT SUPPORT

A ROUGH REPUTATION

I still remember riding the train into San Francisco for my first day at Jawbone. My friend had informally trained me, and now I was leaving the nest and soloing on my first official job in IT. I was this happy hippie with the Jesus beard and long hair, and I wore the only pair of jeans I owned that didn't have a rip in them. I considered myself lucky to have a job, and I was eager to help people. I think I made $25 an hour, which after months of food stamps and co-op living seemed like a fortune to me.

I noticed something odd right away, however. When I told people I worked in IT, most would frown and just shake their heads as if to say, "Bummer man, sorry to hear that." I was perplexed. Here I was starting this cool new profession, and people acted like they felt sorry for me. When I asked why, my friends explained that they hated their IT departments. The IT people were mean and treated them like they were stupid. When they brought in their laptops for help fixing a problem, the IT guys acted annoyed, like they were interrupted from more important work to fix this stupid laptop.

I was surprised, because for me up to that point working in IT was awesome. At Pivotal Labs, we changed RAM blindfolded, staged ping-pong tournaments, and ran around helping people and making friends. At most places, I learned, IT people were not so highly regarded. IT guys were not fighting off the beautiful women, if you know what I mean. When you walked into a restaurant, the maître d' didn't say, "Right this way, sir. We have a table right here. Step aside folks, we have an IT man in the house. Ladies, did you hear someone from IT is in the restaurant tonight?" When you told someone you were in IT, they grimaced and looked away. I got more respect for being an unpublished writer than I did for working in IT.

For the most part, people think of IT workers as socially awkward characters who come from a gaming and computer-nerd culture. They spend a lot of time behind a screen playing *Dungeons and Dragons*. They sit next to each other in bars or cafes Facebooking each other instead of talking. This might not be accurate, but it's certainly the general perception.

Like most stereotypes, there is a hint of truth to this image of the computer tech. IT workers are not expected to have sophisticated social skills. The IT managers who hire them often don't have those skills themselves, so they don't look for qualities like social or emotional intelligence when they hire people for their team. As a result, a lot of people working in IT can't form a genuine connection with the people they help. Many lack basic social graces that can put customers at ease. As a result, they can come across as remote, or even worse, kind of creepy. They can talk for hours with gamers and developers, but they can't carry on a conversation with someone who doesn't share their interests in technology.

Not everyone who works in IT is like that. That said, even those capable of being friendly and engaging with their coworkers often aren't encouraged to behave that way. Their bosses aren't like that, and IT workers' job performance is measured by crunching the most tickets every day rather than how well they interact with the people they help. In short, they don't get credit for providing great customer service.

Part of the problem is the industry's reliance on the Information Technology Infrastructure Library (ITIL), which for thirty-some-odd years has been the primary bible for running IT service management. ITIL is a series of books created by the government in Britain—which might be the most uptight culture on the planet, by the way—and it is heavily focused on process instead of people. With ITIL, success is not measured by customer satisfaction, but by procedural metrics. That may have made sense in the late eighties when ITIL first came out, but the process of implementing ITIL has become a kind of religion. As a consequence, most departments have forgotten that fundamentally the goal of IT support is to do what it takes to make a company's employees as productive as possible, not to be awesome at processes and procedures.

Let's be real. ITIL does not result in mind-blowing customer satisfaction. ITIL includes a customer satisfaction survey, but the results are unscientific and meaningless because it's beyond easy to get a high score. IT departments that rely on ITIL pride themselves on how many certifications they get and how many processes they can implement. They do the processes very well, and this pleases them. However, the actual product we are meant to dish out is IT support to human beings, so shouldn't we make *that* our highest priority?

I think we should, and in Chapter Five, I'll show you the best way to do that.

WELCOME TO THE SERVICE INDUSTRY

When working in IT, support workers understand that

they're there to help people. They also understand that they should be friendly.

What many *don't* understand is that IT is a *service* industry. You don't design products, sell licenses, or launch advertising campaigns. You don't bring in money. You support and serve the folks who do bring in money for the company.

Face it, technology is much simpler today than it was thirty years ago. Computers today are primarily plug-and-play consumer electronics. You can literally rack a server without a screwdriver now. You can build a PC without any special tools. It's not like the seventies when very few people had a computer. Now everyone has a computer in her pocket and knows how to use it.

IT workers need to realize their role today is to serve. Their role should be to wow their customers with beyond-the-call-of-duty help. When you go to a nice restaurant, the waiter doesn't show up at your table and say, "Ugh. I suppose you want something to eat." At a five-star restaurant, the waiter pulls out your wife's chair, spreads a napkin across your lap, presents you with the wine menu, and makes sure you immediately have water. They're ready to tell you not only what the specials are, but also how the chef prepares those specials. Even if you're dining with a large group, everyone's plate hits the table at the same time, and every order is perfect. IT service has to be that good. It may feel demeaning or humbling to some people working in IT, but that's the job today. There's no getting around it.

Today's IT workers need to understand technology, of course, but they also need to know how to relate to people and how to behave in a professional setting.

When I interview candidates for IT jobs, I ask loads of open-ended questions. My psychology training taught me the value of that for understanding what people really think. I wouldn't ask, "Do you get on well with your supervisors?" The candidate can answer that question easily. Instead, I would say, "Tell me about your relationship with your last supervisor." The goal is to get the person to give a deeper answer that reveals their true feelings and attitudes. Social intelligence and attitude are ten times as important as their certifications and how many programming languages they know. If you don't accept that you're in the service industry, you won't last in the socially demanding new world of IT support.

A NEW KIND OF IT WORKER

Spoiler alert: the easiest way to make any IT department better is to hire more women. You're welcome. I know IT managers can't hire based on gender, but from my experience, the ideal ratio for an IT team is half women and half men. It's unfortunate that IT is such a guy's club because women IT workers raise the bar for what work behavior should be.

When I first started at Jawbone, almost the entire company was men—a bunch of male engineers and just a couple of young women in marketing. Then, when we got a huge round of venture capital funding, we beefed up our sales team, and suddenly the office filled with gorgeous women in five-inch heels, fresh out of college. It was remarkable how pretty they all were. I saw this and worried about my team, and rightfully so. Our guys, like most IT types, were not used to interacting with beautiful women.

One day I spotted one of our guys, an intern, sitting with a bunch of these women. He had a dumb smile on his face and was obviously enamored by the attention. We pulled him into an office to have a chat with him. He lived in Oakland and rode the train into the city every day, so I told him, here's our new policy on professionalism: you do not bring your dick to work. When you ride in on the train in the morning and you think you may have brought your dick with you by accident, please drop it off the bridge and pick it up on your way home. We won't have creepy IT guys working here. We are professionals. A little unorthodox, sure, but he got the message.

It's a difficult conversation to have, but it's necessary for your fellow employees to know your IT workers are professionals who act like professionals. IT workers must overcome the stereotype that they are socially awkward, and getting labeled as "creepy" is a death sentence. People already suspect they are nerdy or only interested in helping beautiful women, so even a hint of that kind of behavior confirms their worst assumptions about IT workers. So, don't go there. The second one of your techs makes a coworker uncomfortable, you've lost that customer's trust, and she won't ask for help the next time she needs it.

Most IT workers are well-meaning, smart people who want to do a good job. They can be shy, but they are well-intentioned. The problem is many IT people become jaded over time and start to think of the customer as the enemy. That's the culture they've learned from their bosses over the years, and no one has told them that they should act differently.

I want my IT workers, from interns to senior sysadmins, to have sparkling bedside manners. If they're not approachable, people will not be honest with them, and my IT men and women won't be able to accurately diagnose the problem. If a colleague's trackpad isn't working, it helps to know right away that they spilled a Jack Daniel's and Coke on the keyboard. If you're an IT worker who is rude or awkward, your customers won't trust you, and they won't feel comfortable sharing what happened. You won't know right away what's wrong. It will take you opening the machine and finding a cocktail sloshing around for you to know why the laptop isn't working. Think of yourself as a doctor; if you have no rapport with your patient, they won't be forthcoming about their symptoms, particularly the embarrassing ones, and this makes your job harder.

Good IT support workers are more than just friendly. They must have social skills, and they must have empathy for the customer and the specific work each customer does. They must be sensitive to the deadlines a salesperson has, or the pressures an executive feels, or the crazy creative process a graphic designer uses. IT workers can't just have empathy for nerdy people and just tell nerdy jokes that make references to nerdy movies no one's seen. The job isn't to just fix things. The job is to be approachable and willing to understand what your customers go through. That's the next frontier in IT. That's where IT has to go to be badass.

I don't ask my IT teams to be something they aren't, and I'm not asking you to. Most of the IT people I've met are fun to hang out with outside of work. Many of them are into art or photography or are nationally ranked in computer games. They are interesting, smart people. But for some reason, when they are on the job, many of them feel as if they must act like they can't be bothered.

WHY EMPATHY IS IGNORED

I don't know why, but the worst IT guys seem to get promoted to IT manager. If you've worked in IT, you probably just nodded along with that statement and thought of a few examples right away. Bad IT managers bring their bad habits with them to this higher position, and their attitude trickles down and infects the people under them. These managers might be very good at the process-oriented stuff—the ITIL part of the job—but they don't have the sensibilities or social intelligence to create a customer-focused culture.

Part of the reason for this poor attitude is that IT workers and managers often feel like second-class citizens at their companies. They don't get the same respect, freedom, and acknowledgment as employees or managers in other departments. This creates a cycle of disrespect; people treat IT poorly because *they* feel like IT treats *them* poorly, and IT treats *them* poorly because *they* treat IT poorly. The way to break that cycle is to make sure your IT department practices empathy and other social skills. An IT manager needs to send that message to everyone in the IT department. It takes everyone working together to change this perception.

Developing empathy is a difficult human skill to master—for everyone, not just IT girls and guys. It's easy to care about yourself, but it's challenging to put yourself in other people's shoes. This is why so many relationships don't work out. It's not just a challenge at work; it's a challenge as a human being. Empathy is hard.

Transforming a technology-oriented IT subculture into a human-focused, empathetic subculture is not easy. It flies in the face of all IT has represented for decades. However, if IT workers want the same respect and the same freedom to innovate that the product, sales, and marketing teams get, they must learn empathy for their coworkers. This isn't easy for IT guys who have a chip on their shoulders and have been trained to focus on technical issues, but it's crucial.

When I started at Yahoo!, I could see right away we had a major problem with entrenched IT attitudes about customer service. I thought we could fix it quickly, but this department was so stuck in the mud that we eventually moved every IT manager to other companies because most of them couldn't adapt to the customer-centric model.

Younger people who were new to the profession and not quite jaded yet could see what we were trying to do, and it made sense to them. It was intuitive. If you're nice to people, if you drop everything to help people, and if you show respect for the work they do and the demands they face, you will do a better job and enjoy your work even more. They got it. Many of our old-school IT guys didn't get it, however, and the moment they moved on to other jobs, our customer-service scores all went up significantly. It was a rough transition, but if you're an IT manager in charge of others' livelihoods, you need to either get with the program or update your LinkedIn and move on.

Part of the problem is that no one has ever taught IT workers the importance of social intelligence. I spend a lot of time training people on basic social skills and how to interact with customers in a face-to-face setting. We do role-playing exercises so they can practice greeting people and explaining how they plan to address their customer's problem. It's a revelation for many of them; they've never before been motivated to be empathetic. When the only thing you're judged on is how well you followed the ITIL procedures or how many tickets you handled, you don't pay that much attention to social intelligence. So, I reframe the job for my team members. They learn they need the technical skills *and* the human ones. Boom. Scores go up.

Many talented people can't develop those human skills. To be fair, it's not exactly what most signed up for when they started out in IT. If you have people on your team who can't grasp or develop those human skills, then as IT managers, you must let them go or move them to other jobs where they don't interact with customers. We had a senior technician at one company who was super talented, but he developed a negative attitude over time that began poisoning the whole team. We let him go, which sucks because I love this guy. I've gone to baseball games with him; he's nice, and outside of work, he's a lot of fun. But he was so negative at work that it started killing us. You can't have that on your team, because it hurts everyone and undercuts your achievements. He could fix the shit out of a computer, but his negativity was team poison. When that happens, you need to let them go and hope they learn from it and fix their attitude before their next gig.

THE EFFECT OF IT'S NEGATIVE REPUTATION

Shifting the paradigm from a technical- and process-oriented IT department to one that is customer-oriented is critical to gaining the trust of your company. If IT managers don't have their company's trust, they never get the chance to do cool, innovative stuff, because the company doesn't have enough faith to give them free rein and resources.

Here's an example of how lack of trust can hurt an IT department. One time when I was at Jawbone, the whole company was having trouble printing. None of the printers worked right, and this had become a hot issue that day, because the executives needed to print documents for an upcoming board meeting.

In the lead-up to the board meeting, the CEO had an

executive staff meeting where the product guy talked about products and the sales guy talked about sales and so forth. When it came time for the vice president of IT to give his report, the CEO cut him off. "Listen, Don," the CEO said. "All I want from IT is to be able to fucking print." And then he moved on to the next guy.

This sounds like the CEO is disrespectful, but he was actually one of the best CEOs in the business. The problem was Don's, not the CEO's. Don's problem was that he wasn't tuned in to what his customers wanted and needed. They needed to be able to print. Reasonable, right? When Don can't make that happen, he loses the trust and faith of the CEO. When *that* happens, Don doesn't get to talk about the innovative and cool stuff he wants to do, and he gets chewed out in public. Sorry Don, welcome to IT.

Empathy is understanding what life is like for other people, and Don wasn't taking into consideration how important having reliable printing was to the CEO. Don probably doesn't print much, so having unreliable printers probably didn't seem that important to him. Big mistake. What's most important to his customers is what should be most important to Don. He's forgotten that he's running a customer-service department.

Don shouldn't have been shocked that the CEO had no interest in hearing his excuses for the ongoing problem with printing. When you go to a restaurant and a dish is dirty, you don't want to hear about how the regular dishwasher was out or how a machine malfunctioned. You just want a clean fucking plate.

There's a moral to this story for all IT leaders: Give your customers a voice and listen to it. Fix your shit and fix the things your customers want fixed first. Get in touch with what your *customers* need, not what *you* need. This is why empathy matters.

What happened after the meeting? We installed an amazing new, super-expensive printer that had just been invented, right next to the CEO's desk. No one made a big deal about it, but the message was clear.

We heard you.

IT'S THE SYSTEM, MAN!

Before we go further, it should be said that this job is fucking hard. IT people are, for the most part, good people. Great people, usually. The problem is that the great work an IT department does can be overshadowed by the negative perceptions of a tiny slice of an entire IT department—the help desk. That front line gets all the attention in a company because that's all most people at the company see. Nobody realizes all the other crazy shit IT does in the background. All a customer remembers is the one help-desk employee who was rude.

CONFESSIONS OF THE IT MANAGER

If I were still a therapist, I think I'd specialize in treating CIOs and IT managers. If I did, I imagine I'd hear a lot of the same complaints from each patient, including these:

- ⏻ *We are constantly forced to justify ourselves.* CEOs and other executives often don't see the value IT brings to their companies. In their minds, IT is a cost center and an irritating one at that. When CIOs approach upper-level management for additional resources, they get shot down because CEOs see them as failing in their primary role: providing employee computer support.

- ⏻ *Management doesn't respect us as much as other leaders.* Behind the scenes, IT quietly keeps the company running smoothly. IT fends off hackers, ensures information is protected, and sees to it that transactions are carried out safely and efficiently. All of this is vital to the company's bottom line. However, in high-level meetings, all CIOs hear from other executives is how the frontline IT guy was snarky when he came to upgrade their laptops. These other executives don't understand the value IT brings to the company. They know how much IT *costs*, however, and most of them would say it costs too much.

- ⏻ *The help desk is killing us.* The help desk is the sharpest point of stress for most CIOs. It's usually the worst-performing segment of the overall IT operation, but most CIOs have far more important issues to deal with than to make IT support a priority.

CHALLENGES FACING IT WORKERS

If I were treating IT workers, I'd hear a different set of complaints, such as these:

- ⏻ *We're overwhelmed.* Being a therapist was challenging for me because my clients were deeply troubled and shared their worst problems with me day after day. They were sad, upset, or worried, and they desperately needed my help. As a therapist, it weighed on me. The same thing happens to IT workers. Everyone they talk to has a problem. All day long, alarms go off, people rush around with bulging eyes, and everyone makes demands and never says thank you. Fire drill after fire drill. It weighs on us.

- ⏻ *We're always blamed, even when it's not our fault.* When the internet goes down or people get locked out of the network, they always blame IT, even if IT had nothing to do with it. At one company I worked at, the entire network went down one day without warning. All of a sudden employees popped up out of their cubicles looking angry, confused, or puzzled. "Dude, the network's down! What did you do?" IT at that company wasn't even in charge of the network, but we found the problem and fixed it. Again, this wasn't IT's fault, but when you're an employee sitting at your desk unable to work, who do you blame? That's right: IT.

- ⏻ *You never know when you'll be hit with something big.* One day at Jawbone I heard people yelling inside a conference room. Suddenly the door burst open and an executive assistant ran out crying. I stepped into the conference room and found an executive yelling because he couldn't get the videoconferencing equipment to work. He was pissed off and blamed IT. "It's never worked right," he said. "When will IT get its shit together?" I spent the next two days and nights crawling around on all fours rewiring that conference room. We weren't in charge of the AV system, but we're IT. Yessir, we'll get it fixed!

THIS JOB IS HARD

It's no surprise the pressure on CIOs and IT managers can affect their mental state. The job is so crazy that some people lose their shit.

When I worked at Jawbone, I took over for a guy who one day had just walked away from his desk and never came back. The day I started, they took me to his old desk—my new workstation—and the top was littered with old Rockstar cans. The drawer contained gross old T-shirts and a huge novelty book of matches, both of which were concerning to find on your first day at work. The monitor sat on a ragged egg crate. The computer was locked at the BIOS level, so I couldn't even sign in. This was some super nerdy shit to do, a very IT thing to do. I asked how I could get in touch with my predecessor, so I could get the password.

No one knew. He'd gone out for coffee one day and had never returned. "We're still trying to get our stuff back," the company said. I guess the guy wandered around San Francisco, drinking coffee and chatting with lampposts, and eventually just disappeared into the fog.

We came to think of his condition as "IT madness." It was a joke at first—the idea of IT madness—but as time went on, I began to believe it was a legitimate condition that afflicts people who can't handle the unrelenting stress and thanklessness of a typical IT job. Picture someone sitting in the dark, rocking back and forth, and typing gibberish into a computer. That's IT madness.

I've seen it more than once.

I worked at one company where the IT manager was under a tremendous amount of stress. The vice president of the company put the IT manager on a performance review plan, which is the prelude to firing someone, and the VP micromanaged everything the IT manager did. We loved the IT manager, but the VP hated him, so he set out to make the IT manager's life a living hell. I think he envied how popular the IT manager was.

One day when the vice president, who was Canadian, was on vacation, the IT manager lost it. We're talking pants-on-head crazy, a bona fide case of IT madness.

He sent the VP an email saying something to the effect of "We miss you. There's no one around here to break things when you're gone." Then he told the VP this joke about two Canadians who go camping. While they're in the forest, they play a game of "Twenty Questions." The first Canadian thinks of a noun and tells the second Canadian to ask questions to figure out what he is thinking of. "Is it something you can eat?" the second Canadian asks immediately. The first guy laughs and says, "Sure. I guess you could eat it." So, the second Canadian says, "Is it moose cock?" The IT manager wrote this joke in the email and signed off with something like, "Thanks for being such a dick." He CC'd the entire IT department as well as human resources.

The next day the IT manager came into work as usual and was very promptly escorted out by security.

IT madness like this reflects how difficult the job can be. IT workers are always the first people blamed when something goes wrong. If Amazon Web Services is down, IT gets blamed. If there's a bug in the corporate email server, IT gets blamed. IT workers will be busy with routine work when a hundred people suddenly show up at the door screaming mad. The world is ending, and it's IT's fault.

This is why IT jobs are hard and why IT underperforms.

It's not the IT guy's fault. It's no one's fault. It's the system's fault.

At Jawbone, the first IT job I got on my own, I was this happy hippie and nothing ever fazed me. Then one day a customer hit me with a lot of demands at a time when I was already working on some difficult shit on a very tight deadline. I was under a lot of pressure, and I felt like this woman would not let up. She was not empathetic of my time, and she just rubbed me the wrong way. Finally, I excused myself from her desk, went into a back room, and out of frustration, I kicked the leg off a big IKEA table we had. I broke the leg clean off, and it flew across the room like a perfectly executed field goal.

I felt terrible. I apologized to my coworkers. They were like, "No. It was a good, clean kick!"

Still, they could see I was burnt and our boss started laughing, albeit with a bit of concern. "Oh, no! They got to Ben! They finally broke Brennan!" My boss told me I had to take a week off, no discussion. So, I went down to Guatemala for a week and came back refreshed. When I returned, the team had mounted the broken table leg up on the wall with a sign that said, "Remember, This Job Is Hard."

And that's the point: this job makes people lose it sometimes. Sometimes it even causes IT madness. I know because that one time I was very close to IT madness myself. This job is hard.

FROM A LOSE-LOSE TO A WIN-WIN

The biggest problem with the current system is that it creates a lose-lose-lose situation for everyone—IT workers, customers, and the company.

IT workers lose because they are not empowered to make changes. They aren't trusted to try innovative things. Their ideas are ignored. They're not seen as equals, and this makes the job less appealing to talented people who would excel at it. When you don't feel like a part of the company, when people don't love and respect you, you feel like a slave. You're always told what to do, and no one says thank you. No one should have a job like that.

Customers—your colleagues in the company—lose the opportunity to be more productive and get the tools to make them better at their jobs. If the customers hate getting help from IT, they continue working on broken machines or outdated software, and that cuts into their productivity.

Ultimately, the whole company loses. When a CIO's IT department is weak, the company can face some disastrous screwups. At Jawbone, the company had to recall one of its keynote products in December, right before Christmas, killing that sales cycle. Another company used the same Microsoft Office license for all two thousand employees, and Microsoft sued them for seven figures. Syrians hacked Twitter's website once and planted the Syrian flag there. If you don't have good IT, weird shit like this can affect your bottom line.

If IT managers and CIOs commit to delivering Badass IT Support, everything changes. The rest of the company comes to respect and appreciate the entire IT department. Your most valuable resource—your employees—get better training and equipment and become more productive. You launch more products and ship them faster. As the CIO or IT manager, you get to focus on more important stuff, like negotiating better software deals, finding better virus protection, or designing a wind-powered data center that saves the company a bazillion dollars. When you have Badass IT Support, your IT workers gain credibility and get to work on special projects, like the work-request smartphone apps and automations my teams have created.

Shocker, I know, but when you do IT right, company profits go up. Becoming a Badass IT Support team turns your IT org from a cost center to a value center. Rather than slowing down the talent at your company, a badass IT team will maximize their efficiency and productivity. This results in deadlines being met, products being shipped on time, and shit getting done. Your sales team sells more, your engineers build more, and your company is a better place to work. Happy employees make happy products and have happy customers.

So, if you'd like to get on board with this customer-centric revolution, if you want your team to be not just good, but badass, read on and let's make it happen. When you deliver Badass IT Support, people love you.

Now is a great time to invest in IT support because it's about to get a lot better. Ready to get badass? Let's do this.

PART TWO

DEFINING THE VISION FOR BADASS IT SUPPORT

THE CUSTOMER-CENTRIC PARADIGM SHIFT

Why would anyone write a book called *Badass IT Support*? Why would anyone write a book about IT support at all, for that matter?

As we touched on in Part One, IT has a problem. A big one. The current system is a lose-lose situation for everyone. Well-meaning, talented IT teams get a bad rap, and the people we support are underwhelmed with the service they receive. Change is long overdue.

If change is going to come, however, it will require a complete paradigm shift in how IT workers and managers see their roles.

THE CUSTOMER-CENTRIC REVOLUTION

Technology is our business, and technology has changed. A lot.

Technology has changed in just the last nine years since I got my first job in the field. The iPhone is ten years old for crying out loud!

The customers we support have changed too. They walk around with computers in their pockets with better processors than our desktops used to have. Normal "non-technical" people fall asleep with their laptops next to them in bed. They use computers to watch live TV, book their travel, and talk to their grandma across the ocean. They broadcast live video from their phone. My sixty-year-old mother-in-law has a bitchin' Pinterest wall (nice work, Marsha!). The days when we must teach people how to use computers is long gone.

The result of this huge cultural shift is that our customers no longer need the same kind of help with technology. So, what is an IT worker's role now? What are we good for? How do we provide value to the company? The fortunate—albeit embarrassing—advantage of being so far behind the times is that other industries have figured it out already and can show us what today's customers want.

Facebook, a social media app my grandmother uses, has

better artificial intelligence (AI) than the IT departments at Fortune 500 tech companies. Cable companies pay millions to have Patrick Stewart and Mark Walberg talk about how they listen to customers and improve their customer experience. Cable companies! Instead of renting a car, I use Uber everywhere from Paris to Tokyo. You can pull out your phone and hail a town car in minutes anywhere in the world.

Yet we still operate IT shops like a taxi company. Someone submits a work order, and IT dispatches a tech who shows up in a day or two, and you are required to explain your problem all over again to an annoyed person who seems put out by your request. This is not badass customer service, and it's not what our customers want or deserve. We need to get with the times or find new jobs.

If IT is to thrive in your company, change is inevitable. So, let's get started. It's time to reboot.

TURNING YOUR BRAIN OFF AND ON AGAIN

One guy who has changed the mindset of several IT organizations, ranging from Red Bull to Pabst Blue Ribbon, is Ben Haines, the Obi-Wan Kenobi of IT executives. He once did the dopest thing I've ever seen from a CIO.

When he first came to Yahoo!, Haines was tasked with

turning a twenty-year-old IT culture into a lean, agile org that could restore Yahoo! to its former glory. A year later, Yahoo! was streaming NFL games live in HD, and the company was sold for $4 billion, so you could argue that he knows what he's talking about.

His first month at the company he flew all of his VPs, directors, and managers to Silicon Valley for a leadership summit. Then he put up a slide with just four words on it: *Why are we here?* The answers from his management team were all over the map.

Then Ben did something very simple, followed by something very awesome. I had talked to him beforehand and knew what problem he was trying to solve, so watching it unfold was fascinating. The problem was that our IT org had twenty years (twenty years!) worth of policies, procedures, and services that were either unimportant, outdated, or unnecessary. We would get the transformation he wanted only if we freed everyone's time up from working on the stuff that didn't matter so we could focus on building things that did. In short, we needed to rebuild IT from the ground up.

Haines had arranged for the world's largest whiteboard to be wheeled in, and he had us write down everything we needed to do to keep the company functioning and to accomplish our goals for that year.

"Don't put down what we already do," he said. "Put down what we *need* to do."

Then he said something that a bunch of highly paid, seasoned executives and directors were not very used to hearing: "Now go home and forget everything you know about your job."

After a long pause, and with a bunch of experts in their field speechless, he repeated the order with a little more clarity.

"I'm asking you to go home and forget everything you know about your jobs," he said again. "Forget everything you've ever known about IT. Go home, play with your kids, get drunk, or both. Show up for work on Monday with a clear mind and figure out how we're going to do the things you listed on this board."

That's what I ask you to do for this chapter. Here's why: the way to blow your customers' minds is to understand IT from an outsider's perspective, from your customers' perspective.

That's much easier said than done if you do IT every day for a living. Take a few breaths, clear your head, and forget everything you know, think, or believe about IT support. It's humbling and hard, but it's necessary for transformation. Now, let's take a look at it from our customers' point of view.

Remember, Badass IT Support occurs when *your customers* say you're badass. Saying it about ourselves is the opposite of badass. AC/DC didn't say *Back in Black* had a badass guitar riff; they just played it, and everyone else said it for them. That's when it's real.

THE UX OF IT SUPPORT

Ten years ago, if you asked someone in IT what they did for a living, they'd say, "I fix computers."

Well, congratulations, you just got promoted. Computers are easy to fix now, dude! Your new role, if you want to be the best in your industry, is to create an amazing user experience for your customers.

We're all UX designers now. You may not see yourself as a designer, but you are nevertheless. Think about it: if the customer's user experience doesn't matter, then your company should fire you right now and outsource everything you do to a call center in India. Techs in India can "fix computers" for a lot less than your company pays you.

"But no," you say. "Outsourcing the problem to India is not a good customer experience!" Oh, so customer experience *does* matter, huh?

If it matters, then let's knock it out of the park.

IT managers and support workers need a rudimentary sense of design to create an awesome user experience for their IT customers. They must design every element of IT—from how they set up their office, to how they decorate the space, to how they greet customers. Think about what the experience will be like for customers when they walk in to get help. It's like when you download an app and you can use it right away, without any confusion or uncertainty. You know intuitively how to use it, and the simplicity and elegance of it are seamless. That's how you want your IT operation to be designed. That's what you want your customer experience to be.

If your current office is dark, like a dungeon, smells funky, has old computers stacked everywhere, and has a rat nest of cables sitting on top of old filing cabinets, how excited do you think your customers are to step into it? If the IT workers wear stained T-shirts and are listening to throbbing, high-speed metal, will your customers feel welcomed?

If your current design isn't serving your customers well, it's on you to design it differently. Do you have art on the wall? Are you playing cool music? Is the place well lit? Is there a comfortable place for people to sit while they wait?

An awesome user experience might require other changes as well. What's the voice on your voicemail? Is it fun and on brand with your company? Is it friendly, and does it provide useful information? Or is it some disembodied computer voice that frustrates people and makes them think there isn't a human being behind the message?

When someone emails you with a problem and you have an automated response acknowledging the receipt of the email, is it friendly and encouraging, or is it bland and machinelike? What does that email formatting look like? What happens when people walk in? Does anyone greet them? Is it clear to them they are in the right place? Do they get some idea of how long they will be there before someone says something to them?

People often don't think of these details as "design," but they are all a huge part of the customer experience of interacting with your IT department. You design your customer's user experience whether you realize it or not. Great UX design doesn't just happen on its own. If you don't take the time to consider these things, your IT department probably has a shitty design.

So, how do you design a badass customer experience? It's easier than you might think.

MAKING A BADASS CUSTOMER EXPERIENCE PRIORITY NUMBER ONE

As a consultant who has written core values for several

teams over the years, I've noticed two things: badass customer experience is the only value people remember, and it's the only value that changes the culture.

Providing a badass customer experience must be your highest priority.

Here's why: This core value tells you what the priority is in every decision. Also, it's subversively black and white. Sure, badass is a subjective term. But anyone can pick "badass" out of a lineup nine times out of ten. Flea from the Chili Peppers is a badass bass player. No musician will disagree with that. Ever listened to Led Zeppelin, taken a first-class Virgin Atlantic Flight, or experienced the service at the St. Regis on Third Street in San Francisco? All badass. No one who has experienced these would disagree. Badass is universal.

When IT workers provide Badass IT Support, the customer's experience is the focus of everything those support workers do. Every employee at the company is our customer, and everything IT managers and workers do is directed at making them happy and productive. If your department does something that doesn't serve that central goal, stop doing it. If there is a way to provide better service, adopt it.

At Yahoo!, I made customer service one of the seven core values of our IT department, and to be honest, it's the only one that stuck through the years. I made it very clear: "Truly badass customer experience is always priority one." Everything we did had to go through that filter.

Here's an example: At one point before I worked there, Yahoo! eliminated email as a way customers could contact IT. Don't ask me why. The only way to contact IT at this ten-thousand-plus-person, Fortune 500 company was by phone, in person, or through chat, and wait times for those channels were up to forty-five minutes! It made no sense to take away a customer's freedom to send an email about their problem. Why not let them shoot us an email instead of sitting on hold for forty-five minutes, unable to accomplish anything? It baffled me and every one of our customers.

The first week I was there, we had an all-hands meeting with the CIO at Yahoo!. Hundreds of people were there, and the CIO talked about making IT more attuned to customer needs. I loved it. At one point, the CIO asked, "By the way, why can't we email IT when we need help at this company?" I thought, "Sweet! Same page. Let's do it."

Not everyone liked the idea. After the CIO's talk, I went up to one of my colleagues and mentioned I was pleased that management wanted better customer service from IT. This guy I talked to was one of our star employees—a fantastic worker and very well respected—and I liked him.

He was tall with braces and glasses—super-duper nerdy but also very funny. Most of the time.

"I loved what he said about email," I told my colleague. "Let's bring it back. Let's do this."

What I didn't realize was that this guy had been in charge of eliminating email support in the first place. He'd spent months spinning down email, deactivating the account, and rerouting everything to phone and chat support.

He turned red and trembled. A lot. I mean, I thought his braces were going to fly off and take out innocent bystanders. I took a step back. I thought this was a bona fide case of IT madness surfacing right before my eyes.

"There is no way we're bringing email back," he said through clenched teeth. Uh oh, shit was getting real.

"Uh, that's what the CIO just said," I replied. "He's your boss's boss's boss's boss. I don't think you get to choose. Plus, it's a no-brainer—it's better for everyone."

"No. It. Isn't," he said, his voice rising dangerously. "It's not better, and we're not letting you do it."

Holy shit. A crowd began to gather. It was unusual for this good-natured guy to yell.

He kept the fight up for weeks—until he got kicked off the email-restoration project by a vice president who tired of him sabotaging a major initiative.

Later, I talked to him about why he got so mad. I had to know. I think it was because he had spent so much time removing email that it killed him to see that work wasted. He dove so deep he could not get back to the surface to see that the idea didn't help our primary goal of making it easier for customers to get our help.

For him, it was all about the process, I think, but he was forgetting what the process was there to accomplish in the first place. This mindset happens often in ITIL, where the processes become a kind of cult or religion, where the religion becomes so focused on the rituals that it forgets it was there in the first place to bring peace and love to the world.

IT AS A SERVICE INDUSTRY

It's important to remember that IT exists to provide a service. A lot of people in IT forget that's what we're here for.

Working in the service industry, in a restaurant or behind a bar, is like getting an MBA in customer relations. Even when people yell at you, you must smile and deliver them hot, delicious food and a perfect martini because you work for tips. You must be at their beck and call and put up with all their demands because you need tips to pay the rent. I worked in the service industry for three years during grad school, and it taught me humility to say the least. It also taught me that the better the service, the better the tips. Even though I no longer work for tips, that lesson has stayed with me all these years, and I use that mentality all the time now. If you are in IT, you are there to serve; you must get that through your head to be successful.

Steve Jobs is famous for saying, "Real artists ship." That meant you can have all kinds of artistic ideas, but if you aren't developing those ideas into a product that can ship, you aren't a real artist. He even called the people who worked on Apple products "artists" instead of "engineers." I think this is notable because the most user-friendly operating system and retail stores in the world came from people who viewed themselves as artists and designers, not technicians or engineers.

When you're in IT, you must think about yourself that way and design an experience that blows customers away.

Many IT departments fall short on this front because of their devotion to ITIL. ITIL, which we talked about in Chapter One, stands for the Information Technology Infrastructure Library. ITIL sets out all the accepted and detailed practices for IT service.

Some people think they are successful because they have implemented all of ITIL's Key Performance Indicators (KPI), such as how many work request tickets they've closed and the average time it took to close them. But, like I said before, ITIL, KPIs, and SLAs (Service Level Agreements, or your goal for how long it will take you to fix a problem) have almost nothing to do with customer service. They are all just processes and procedures. Nevertheless, a lot of neckbeardy IT professionals are devoted to them and have built their careers on carrying them out.

KPIs and SLAs are worthwhile in that they are an attempt to measure success. They are established by the IT department without any input from customers, however. Consequently, KPIs and SLAs don't measure the important things like customer satisfaction and customer experience.

When I'm in IT circles and mention that ITIL is outdated and useless, people either walk away or get straight-up aggressive. IT people don't like it when I tell them ITIL is a culture focused on the process and not the people. When you get too focused on the culture, you forget the very thing the processes are supposed to accomplish. You've created a church that worships the religion and not the god the religion is based on, which in this case is a badass customer experience.

ITIL teams say they are there to support the business, the

money-making entity they work for. Badass IT teams think of IT as the business, a business with a product, brand, and customers of its own. The product is Badass IT Support, the customers are the employees of the company, and the brand is trust, respect, and goodwill. Jay-Z once said, "I'm not a businessman. I'm a business, man." I think of IT the same way. We're not helping a business. We are a business.

The other problem with ITIL and ITIL teams is that all this process keeps IT from moving at the speed of the business we're meant to support. They don't make employees more productive. That's the main reason why we see Shadow IT, every IT department's nemesis, increasing every year. Speaking of which...

SHADOW IT

If you don't work in IT, you may have never heard this term, but IT managers know it all too well. Shadow IT is like a black market for IT products. Black markets spring up when governments can't or won't provide what the citizens want. Similarly, Shadow IT shows up when departments within a company get so sick of waiting for IT to provide a service that they go out and buy the service for themselves. They set it up and run it themselves because it helps them do their jobs better. They often don't even tell IT when they do it.

IT people death-hate Shadow IT because it's neither secure nor safe. If IT isn't managing the data, sensitive company information is handled by people who are not system administrators, and this makes it vulnerable to hackers. It can be disastrous. Picture a human resources department setting up an unprotected Shadow IT system with all their employees' Social Security numbers, addresses, and checking account numbers on it. Hackers drool when they spot shit like that.

What does Shadow IT say about your IT department? If IT managers have other departments throwing up their hands and spending their department's budget on their own IT, that means your IT department has failed them. If you can't do your job well enough to get that department what it needs, something's broken. You can't blame the people in that department for wanting to do their jobs. They asked you for this two years ago, and you never did it, so they finally just said, "Fuck it. We've got a job to do. Let's get the IT we need." I don't think it says something bad about the company when one of its departments resorts to Shadow IT; I think it says something bad about the IT department.

If your IT department spots Shadow IT, look inward and ask what part you played in the breakdown. Once you've done that, it's time to ask yourself things like, "What can we do differently so people don't feel they need to go around us?"

What customers today need is that next-level support. They need that soft touch, that white-glove service and help with the bigger, more complex issues. They've changed, but ITIL and the IT departments that worship it haven't kept up with the needs of the business.

Technology is not the hard part anymore. What's hard is combining knowledge of technology with social intelligence and applying those two things with empathy to everyone in your company. Shadow IT is proof our customers have changed and now feel empowered. As an IT guy, you can bitch about this recent development, or you can admit you're late to the party. You can admit you work ridiculously slow and need to step up your game. It's a hard pill to swallow, but Shadow IT is our fault, whether we admit it or not.

THE IMPORTANCE OF VISION

When you work in IT, you make hundreds of micro-decisions a day. How do I word this email? How do we communicate this big change to the network? How do we let people know about an upcoming outage? What kind of questions will people have, and how can we consistently answer those questions? How do we train our technicians? Do we wear uniforms?

Vision captures the macro-idea, and through that, it informs all of these microdecisions.

IT managers and CIOs can be inspired by things and daydream about them, but vision comes into play when they manifest those inspirations and create their own reality from them. Vision is carrying out an idea in real life. Vision is creating something that's never been done before and then watching as other people copy it until it seems like such an obvious solution that people wonder why it wasn't created years sooner.

The Genius Bar at Apple is a classic example. Before the Genius Bar, you brought your broken computer into some dark storefront in a rundown strip mall and explained your problem to some grumpy, underpaid guy in wrinkled pants who stared at your girlfriend's boobs while you talked. Then he took your computer and kept it for a week and lost all your data because he wasn't good at his job to begin with.

That's what IT was like for a lot of people until, boom, here come Apple stores with their Genius Bars. Now you can walk into a clean, inviting place and talk to a friendly, meticulous person wearing a clean T-shirt uniform who is happy to see you and stoked about teaching you about Macs. These are not techs trained in ITIL. These are smart people who've gone through Apple's specialized training and been certified to fix your problem with style.

Steve Jobs wouldn't set up shop in a dingy strip mall next

to a laundromat. His team created their own training and certification, which was as much about teaching communication skills as it was about anything else. Apple even trained its people how to deliver bad news to a customer. At Apple, you were trained never to use the word "unfortunately." For instance, a normal IT professional might say, "*Unfortunately*, we can't figure out your problem. We sent it to the master technician to look at." If you worked at Apple, you'd say, "*As it turns out*, you've got an interesting issue going on, so let's have our master technician look at your Mac!" By using "as it turns out" rather than "unfortunately," it doesn't sound like such bad news.

Apple was also the first IT shop I know of that adopted Net Promoter Score (NPS®). We'll talk more about that later in the book, but the NPS is an index that measures how much customers will recommend your product to others. It's the same index the Ritz Carlton and other companies that excel in customer service use. Every single company I've worked for has had a manager or an executive come back from the Apple Store and say, "Why don't we have a Genius Bar?" Using NPS rather than traditional CSAT measures is a big reason why Apple's customer experience blows everyone away. All of these details came from a simple vision from Apple that has been copied by every company since.

FINDING YOUR INSPIRATION

Well, you can have a Genius Bar—or at least something like it—pretty easily. The Genius Bar is not your vision. It's your inspiration. It's great to be inspired by other influences, but ultimately IT managers must also create their own vision from that inspiration.

Walk into your own crappy (or not crappy, whatever) IT department, and close your eyes. Imagine what the most amazing customer experience would look like and form your vision from that. Then reverse engineer the whole thing and make it happen.

What if we had this awesome check-in system where people could badge-in and their picture would come up, and they could see where they were in the line of customers? What if we made it our practice to greet everyone the second they walked in and assure them we'll be with them shortly? What if we had music playing? What if we had cool couches so customers could be comfortable if they had to wait?

Vision gives your people a roadmap. You can't just tell your IT folks to go out there and be awesome. If there is no vision, there is no goal. If there is no clear goal, there is no motivation. Paint the picture for them with an awesome vision so they can execute it for you every day.

EARNING YOUR CUSTOMERS' RESPECT

A customer-centric vision develops a mutual respect between IT and the customer, and between IT and the rest of the company as well. When you're empathetic, you do a better job. People respect you more. It changes the company dynamic; instead of the company being the business and you being the cost center, IT becomes a valued partner.

Having the new vision is a win-win-win across the board. Your IT department is respected. The IT girls and guys have more fun at work. Your customers see you as rock stars, not enemies. It's a win for your career.

The customers win because it feels good to have a friendly IT environment. Your customers' jobs are hard, and badass IT techs can brighten their day even when other things go bad.

The benefit of a customer-centric approach can be huge for the company. The company meets more deadlines, and its workers are more productive. An IT team that's well-liked and respected feels empowered to do fun, innovative things. For instance, at Twitter, we had a hack week, and one team made a Marauder's Map inspired by a Harry Potter book. People who opted in could have their cell phones triangulated through the office Wi-Fi. We were in a new, huge building at the time, and the map made it easier to find where anyone was in real time. At Yahoo!, we designed a unified video conferencing system for our conference rooms and rolled it out for the whole company worldwide in one weekend. That's a very difficult thing to accomplish, but we'd earned credibility and were trusted with money for big projects like that.

These are the cool things that come your way when you provide Badass IT Support. But you won't get there unless you raise the bar for what IT Support should be.

The point of having badass customer experience as your primary core value is that every conversation—beginning, middle, and end—is focused on the customer. That central value gives IT departments a shared language to talk about work, make decisions, and set goals.

When IT managers and CIOs have a badass vision and are crystal clear about their goals, decisions begin to make themselves. This is where the real power of transformation starts to take hold.

Read on to find out how to make that happen and raise the bar at your company.

LET'S RAISE OUR OWN BAR

Sadly, most IT departments have zero motivation to raise the bar for how awesome IT support should be. Why should they? Companies only have one IT department, so employees—the customers—have no choice in the matter. As I pointed out early in this book, if you don't like Uber, you can switch to Lyft. If the service sucks at one restaurant, you can go to another one. As IT departments, however, we have a monopoly. Employees must use their company's IT department even if it sucks. This lack of competition and motivation to be awesome has resulted in a very low bar for IT support. Our customers have gotten used to this by now, and people generally expect IT to be underwhelming. They've just accepted it. It is what it is.

IT managers and workers who want to enjoy their jobs and earn the respect of their colleagues can raise the bar themselves, however. It's the only way to become badass, and as we'll talk about in this chapter, it's easy, it's a lot more fun, and there's already a playbook for it. The steps are straightforward. First, define what Badass IT Support means for your company. Second, throw down the gauntlet and challenge yourself to let *your customers* measure your performance. When your customers say you're badass, then you're badass. They get to choose. It's only when *they* call you badass that you know it's true. In this chapter, I'll tell you why it's going to be a lot easier than you think. The good thing about IT being so behind the times in providing awesome customer-centric support is that other industries have already blazed the trail for us. We'll talk about innovating later, but right now, IT just needs to catch up!

You hear all the time how a company aims to provide "world-class" service or a "world-class" product, but the term "world-class" has been overused so much that it doesn't mean anything anymore. There is no way to numerically or scientifically quantify what "world-class" means, because there's no shared metric everyone agrees on.

That's why I use the term "Badass IT Support." Unlike "world-class," the word "badass" still means something. Badass IT folks are people who get the job done, against all odds. They kick ass, they make the impossible happen, and, most importantly, they do it with style.

Real excellence should be measured by tangible results that matter to the people we support. The ITIL playbook has loads of key performance indicators and metrics that our customers couldn't give two shits about, like how many tickets you closed last week. Our customers don't care how many other people we helped; they care about *their* experience.

Every company I've consulted for and taught the QSTAC™ method, a customer-service-based survey I describe in Chapter Five, has promptly thrown their traditional metrics out the window and adopted QSTAC as the golden metric.

Why? Because put simply, the traditional performance indicators are ineffectual at transforming the customer experience. I remember at Twitter we tracked the number of tickets closed and had a contest. We had a bunch of uber-smart techs and sysadmins, but the intern won the contest every time. He ran around giving people keyboards and mice and wrote out a ticket for each one. Naturally, it looked like his performance was off the charts compared to the rest of us, but that wasn't an accurate picture. There is no correlation between the number of tickets closed and badasss customer experience. Let's be real, if IT was on top of its game, there wouldn't be any tickets at all; everything would just work.

Customer satisfaction comes from individual badass

customer experiences. Sometimes those experiences, like a systemic problem with the network, last three weeks. Sometimes they last a millisecond, such as a chat bot that tells you what you need without requiring that you contact IT. When you nail each of these individual customer experiences every time, that's when you've won.

WHAT DO YOUR CUSTOMERS WANT?

Badass IT Support involves finding out what your customers want and then kicking the shit out of it. There's even a hack If you don't have specific feedback about it. Just ask yourself: "Is this badass?" Let's try it.

Telling someone to just turn it off and on again? Not badass. Creating a bot that answers common questions in milliseconds on any device? Badass.

Thirty-minute chat wait times? Not badass. Live chat with a zero-second wait time? Badass.

Dingy IT help desks that look like the DMV or a bodega in a bad neighborhood? Not badass. Making your IT area the most comfortable place in the office to hang out with dope music playing, cool art on the walls, and comfortable seating where anyone can lounge around, and execs can hide from their assistants and chiefs of staff? Badass.

Badass is subjective in theory, but in practice, it's pretty black and white. That's why it's dope. That's why it's real. That's why it works. It's subjective in the best way. You know it when you see it. It's like courage. "Courage" is a subjective term, but you know it when you see it, and you never mistake it with cowardice. I've lived in three countries and traveled throughout the US, Europe, Asia, and Central America. There are a lot of cultural differences, but I did notice that courage was valued by all these cultures. Being nice wasn't always valued. Eye contact wasn't either. Hygiene certainly wasn't always valued. But courage was universally seen as the right thing to have in every culture.

World-class? Fuck that. "World-class" is a watered-down term that doesn't mean anything anymore and is seen by most consumers these days as a desperate, empty boast. If you're telling everyone how "world-class" you are, then you are not world-class.

"Badass," on the other hand, is unadulterated and true. An amazing blues guitarist shredding at 3:00 a.m. in an after-hours club smoking a cigarette and playing licks you've never heard is badass. Jimmy Hendrix, Conor McGregor, the list goes on. All badass without debate.

But many businesses are badass too. The Four Seasons hotel. The St. Regis on Third Street in San Francisco.

Zappos. What do these all have in common? They all provide a badass customer experience, and their customers all swear by those companies and are fiercely loyal to them.

GOING ABOVE AND BEYOND

Being badass means you surprise and delight your customers. At Jawbone, for instance, we took a few extra steps when we switched everyone over from PCs to Macs to make this painful process a lot of fun.

Normally when you get a new computer at work, the techs pull it out, image it, install software, and hand you the new machine. At Jawbone, we tweaked these details to surprise and delight our employees, and it was a big hit. First, we carefully pulled out each computer, got it completely ready to log into, and then slid the computer back into the original plastic film and taped the box back up so it looked brand new. We bought huge red bows with our own money, and we put them on the boxes and set them out on everyone's desk the night before the big changeover. We even had their wireless keyboards and mice all charged, paired, and ready to go. When people came in the next morning, it was like a holiday. It was a lot of extra work, but it was badass.

None of this was in anyone's job description, but we wanted to go above and beyond. Our team had a whiteboard in our IT offices at Jawbone, and we wrote on it in big letters, "Were you awesome today?" People even started calling us Team Awesome. The head of engineering gave our intern the nickname Junior Awesome. That was our brand. We didn't make it up; people called us that on their own, and they weren't sarcastic for a change.

When you focus on the customer and deliver Badass IT Support, you always look for ways to make IT a little more fun. At one company, we had a dice game set up, and we called it The High Roller Game. Everyone in the company would stop by to play, even if they didn't need any IT help. One woman got the nickname High Roller because she won so many times, and she still calls herself that years later. We did that just because it was fun. It led to Badass IT Support as well because it allowed us to get to know our customers better, and they got to know us better. This made people more comfortable when approaching us for help and made IT an awesome team to be on.

DAMN, THAT WAS FAST! AN EXAMPLE OF BADASS IT SUPPORT

At Jawbone, my first order of business was moving the entire company over from Windows to Macs, as I mentioned earlier. Of course, the instant that I did that, Apple announced a new product, the MacBook Air. It was light, shiny, and sexy looking, and everybody had to have one.

Never mind that it was a total piece-of-shit laptop—there was almost no storage, no backlit keyboard, and only one USB port—every executive in Silicon Valley needed it yesterday. You can't meet your CEO buddies for forty-dollar martinis and be the only one at the table without the new MacBook Air! I think not! That would be like wearing a cell phone holster or not owning a Tesla!

A note about Jawbone. Jawbone was cool because it had two founders. Also, Jawbone sucked because it had two founders. I kid! They were both amazing guys that everyone, including our team, loved. As such, we pulled strings with our Apple friends to get them two of the first MacBook Airs in Silicon Valley.

The laptops arrived at our offices in San Francisco just before the close of business one day. The problem was that one of our founders lived in London and was leaving the next day for Asia. He needed the MacBook Air for his trip, and we needed to find a way to get the new machine set up and shipped to him on time.

My coworker Bill and I discussed the situation.

"Obviously it's impossible at 5:00 p.m. to image a computer, send it after hours across seven time zones, and have it arrive on our founder's doorstep right before he hops into his town car and heads to the airport, right?" I asked.

"Yup," Bill said.

"I mean, it's like literally impossible, right?"

"Yup."

"But we're gonna do it anyway, right?"

"Yup," Bill said again.

He's a man of few words, that Bill. I hauled ass back to the lab and started ghosting an image onto the machine while Bill researched the shipping possibilities. He was pretty connected in SF, and after making a few calls, he strolled back in with a big smile.

"OK, so there's this service where a courier will pick up a package and literally take it *onto* the tarmac at SFO and throw it on the next FedEx plane to London," he said.

"No shit. How much?"

"Fucking expensive."

"So, we're gonna do it?"

"If you can have it ready in twenty minutes."

Eighteen minutes later, the laptop was ready to go. The elevator bell dinged, and a greasy-looking guy with a motorcycle helmet popped out on our floor. We handed him the laptop and asked when the last flight left that night.

"Twenty-five minutes," he said, glancing at his watch.

"Dude, you going to make it?" I asked.

"Yup."

Another man of few words, I guess. If you've ever seen the lane-splitting motorcycles flying past you on the 101, you won't be surprised that thirty minutes later our phones buzzed with a FedEx notification that our parcel was on its way to an on-time delivery in London.

The next day I got a call from a +44 international number. I had a good idea who it was.

"How the fuck did you guys get that laptop here?" our founder in London shouted.

"Dude, we're happy to help," I said.

"You guys are seriously badass."

His words, not ours. When *they* say it, that's when it counts.

THE POWER OF EMPATHY

You won't find a section on it in any ITIL manual, but a key characteristic of Badass IT Support is empathy—the ability to put yourself in the shoes of others. That's not an easy thing to learn.

I spent thousands of hours counseling people as a psychotherapist, and having empathy was a daily challenge even for me. It still is. I strive every day to have empathy because it's such an important human skill. It's essential if you want to run a customer-centric organization.

Understanding your customers and consulting with them about their needs brings what I call "light bulb moments" that tell you what to include in your IT design. Some people call them aha moments. These simple insights can make a huge difference and show you things about your service you would never have noticed on your own.

For example, at Yahoo!, our first customer survey indicated that a lot of people felt they were ignored when they first walked into the IT areas. Our people were quite friendly and charming when they helped people, but when a customer first walked in, for some reason no one said anything to them. Some customers weren't even sure they were in the right place and would just walk back to their desks confused. Our guys didn't realize this was a problem, even though by all accounts this had been the norm for years.

Immediately after getting this customer's feedback, we trained our technicians to greet everyone immediately. It was simple and obvious, but we had previously overlooked it. We also trained them to slow down and actively listen to customers and let them fully explain what they think might be causing their problem. We taught them to resist the urge to think they always knew what was right and what was wrong. Our customer satisfaction scores went up immediately after we started this, just because our technicians started saying "Hi." Who knew?

TALKING CUSTOMERS THROUGH A SOLUTION

Another thing we learned from our first survey at Yahoo! was how important it was to talk people through what we did as we fixed their equipment. I cannot overstate the importance of this. When a customer comes in with a problem with their phone, for instance, well-meaning technicians need to resist the urge to grab the customer's phone and start pushing buttons and swiping through screens. This makes customers very nervous, and for good reason! The support person might only be in the settings, but the customer might think the tech is going through the customer's private collection of cat videos or who knows what. That was another light bulb moment for us; our guys read that feedback and agreed they wouldn't want a stranger poking around on their phone either. Empathy was achieved, and the customer no longer had to sit there nervously while an IT guy did god knows what to their iPhone.

The idea here is that it's important to *show* the customer what you do and explain *why* you do it. We taught our techs to think out loud, which took some getting used to for sure. "OK, now I'm uninstalling the VPN client and reinstalling it to see if that fixes the problem." Then the customer has a chance to chime in and ask questions or make sure you know to save his open browser tabs. This builds trust and lowers anxiety. Talking them through the process also helps make the time go by faster for the customer. It makes her feel like you're on a journey to fix her issue together. That experience is infinitely more fun than standing there in silence while some stranger clicks around in your private shit.

LISTEN TO YOUR CUSTOMERS

Being badass and customer-centric means you let customers measure your value. A prerequisite to this is being ready to listen intentionally and effectively. The next chapter is all about how to give your customers a clear voice and a seat at the planning table. This is what being customer-centric is all about.

The tool I invented years ago to give my clients' customers a voice is called QSTAC™, which we'll talk about later in the book. This tool is custom-tailored to this customer-centric ideal. I spent months researching and designing it, analyzing white papers and studying research methods. We used it at Yahoo! and several other companies with great success. Customers taking the survey not only gave us numerical scores for our work, but they shared comments and feedback to help explain the scores' context and how to fix what was broken.

The QSTAC gave us far better results than any ITIL metrics could because it measured only one thing: how badass our customers felt we were. And it measured the hell out of it. The QSTAC survey creates an internal motivation to raise the bar, to be the best. As a manager, you can see who provides great customer service and who provides customer service that's just okay, and you can modify your strategy accordingly, so everyone is kicking ass. In large companies, that also sets up some healthy competition among internal IT teams. More about the QSTAC later. For now, I want to connect with you, the reader. Let's check in, shall we?

A QUICK CHECK-IN

I wrote this book for you, and it means the world to me that you've made it this far. I'm also excited because you're in luck. We're about to kick it into gear and the book is about to start rocking and rolling. You've made it, you're halfway done, and I assure you this book is about to really get cooking.

The journey to becoming a Badass IT Support team is something that you and your team will never forget. In the four parts of this book, my goal is to give you all the tools you need to do on your own what other companies have paid me more than a hundred thousand dollars each to do for them. Part One was an intro to myself and to the state of IT support today. Part Two stayed super high level with the philosophy of customer centricity and why we have to raise our own bar and hold ourselves to a badass standard of excellence if we want to reach our potential.

Part Three gets more granular and tells you exactly what you need to have in place to start your journey. Then comes Part Four. I fucking love Part Four. That's where shit gets real, where we get down and dirty in the weeds and talk about how to execute every step of the way. In Part Four, we'll talk about how to execute on the easy parts, the hard parts, and then my favorite: the fun parts, building dope shit and paying it forward to our fellow IT professionals.

Are you ready? Of course, you are! You're a badass! That said, you've made it halfway through, so take a break, pour a glass of whiskey, or boil a pot of tea, and come back when you're ready. The next two parts of this book contain everything I have learned about building badass teams at company after company. I've built a great career on this knowledge and cannot wait to share it with you. Here comes the good shit. Let's get badass.

PART THREE

WELCOME TO BADASS

GIVING YOUR CUSTOMER A VOICE

Transforming a team isn't easy. Awesome things rarely are. That said, if you're up to the challenge, Badass IT Support is achievable at any company.

Over the years I've developed a streamlined, proven playbook that anyone can use to transform their team into a badass, customer-centric org that blows your customers' minds. The formula isn't rocket surgery (think about it). It's simple and straightforward: give your customers a clear voice and shape your strategy by what they say. Once you've responded to your customers' voice, measure your performance empirically to see if what you're doing is blowing your customers' minds or if you need to change tactics. Rinse and repeat. We'll talk about that in Chapter Six, so hang tight. For now, let's focus on the most important thing: how to listen to your customers.

CHOOSING A SURVEY

You may think that learning what you need to fix to become the perfect IT team is a daunting task. It's actually incredibly simple if you have the right tool. What's more, your customers will do all the work for you! *Phew*, right? Your only job is to give them a clear voice and listen to it. Put those guys to work for once!

So how do you give customers this crystal clear voice? As much as it pains me to say, and it pains me greatly, it turns out the only real way to give your customers a voice is a [*wince!*] survey. Sorry.

I fucking hate surveys. I hate taking them, and I hate sending them. They drive me bonkers. They all seem so basic and unscientific because they are.

That's why we created our own survey, called the QSTAC. I remember in grad school getting it drilled into my head how self-report data, aka surveys, are the worst kind of data that exists. Surveys are unreliable at best, misleading at worst, and always open to interpretation. Survey data is what you use when you have no other option.

To top it off, the surveys that IT support teams have used for decades, mathematically speaking, absolutely suck; the data is so easily manipulated and so open to interpretation that the results are rendered meaningless. If your data sucks, your response to that data will suck. Garbage in, garbage out. Without accurate, actionable data, your survey will never result in Badass IT Support. It will only serve to waste everyone's time and result in more of the same, quarter after quarter.

Okay, so surveys suck, but we have to use them anyway? Yep. IT leaders traditionally have had a choice of several established survey formats, namely CSAT, NPS, or CES. We'll dive into what each of those stands for shortly. The problem with those surveys is they are either misleading— making you look better than you are—or don't deliver the actionable information an IT org needs to improve.

The worst of the bunch is the one most often used by IT departments—the CSAT, which stands for customer satisfaction. It's old and it's been used for years, but it doesn't accurately measure satisfaction meaningfully and is easy to manipulate. For those outside of IT, we'll quickly summarize how the CSAT works.

After a customer gets off the phone with IT, a survey asks the customer about his interaction. Was the customer very satisfied, satisfied, not satisfied, or completely unsatisfied? Sometimes it simply asks if you were "satisfied" or "not satisfied." It's easy and benign and categorically unscientific.

The main problem is there is no distinction between "very

satisfied" and "satisfied." Both ratings give you a score of 100. A team doing the bare minimum can get the same score as a team blowing every customer's mind. Leaving your customer merely "satisfied" is not badass. It's the antithesis of badass. A great score on the CSAT might make your team look good to your corporate overlords, but it doesn't separate the amazing from the good, and it is in no way a measure of overall badassery.

If CSAT were an accurate measure, then why do so many IT departments suck? If CSAT were doing its job and motivating a team to be better, we'd have better IT teams. But we don't. I know because I've built career-transforming teams who used the CSAT for years and were still underperforming.

"DUDE, WE ALREADY HAVE A SURVEY"

This is a common variation of my favorite, quintessential IT manager catchphrase: "We tried that already." Every time I start a consulting gig, without fail, a manager will pull me aside and say, "Brennan, we're already using a survey." I always try to act like I've never heard that response and do my best to not burst out laughing while they're midsentence. I'm rarely successful at this. "Awesome! That's great to hear. So, you are already a world-class, best-in-industry org that blows everyone's minds at your company? Is your team the best there is? If so, *mazel tov!* You won't be needing my services then."

If not, I'll say, "Then maybe—just maybe—the survey you use doesn't give you the best data. If your survey data is not actionable enough to help make you the best in the industry, why waste your employees' time?" Hand to god, I've worked at multiple companies that didn't even read the results of the survey they sent out every quarter. That speaks volumes. Respect your employees' time and your own, and choose a survey that makes a difference.

DEATH BY ACRONYM: NPS VS. CSAT VS. CES VS. QSTAC

There are four types of surveys out there at our disposal, an alphabet soup of deadly acronyms. My apologies. I'll make it quick. If you're bored out of your mind, I've included a chart that summarizes everything. You can check it out and then skip to the next section if you want. No worries! I feel your pain. Death by acronym is real, not to mention a known symptom of IT madness.

	CSAT	NPS®	CES	QSTAC™
Stands For	Customer Satisfaction	Net Promoter Score®	Customer Effort Score™	**Q**uality **S**peed **T**echnical Knowledge **A**pproachability **C**ommunication
Used By	All IT teams and traditional companies who haven't yet adopted NPS®	Apple, Ritz Carlton, Audi, Zappos, IBM	Marketing and sales orgs. Recommended by *Harvard Business Review*. Ridiculed as unnecessary by other sources	IT teams going for best-in-industry, world-class customer service
The Philosophy	Important to keep the customer "satisfied."	Fiercely loyal customers (promoters) grow your business.	Reducing customer effort necessarily increases loyalty.	Badass is the new "good."
The Question	How satisfied were you with your interaction with IT?	How likely are you to recommend us to a friend?	How easy did the organization make it for me to handle my issue?	Rate your IT Team on...
The Calculation	Simple average. CSAT score is the percentage of respondents who said "satisfied" or above.	NPS® = % of promoters minus % of detractors.	Simple average. A high score indicates your company is easy to interact with.	Points for awesome, no points for good, points off for average or below
Actionable?	Somewhat. It helps identify individual employees who are providing bad experiences.	Super informative, but not very actionable.	Super actionable in that it shows areas of difficulty.	Incredibly actionable
Limitations	Data is not particularly meaningful or scientific. Doesn't differentiate between "good" experiences and "awesome" experiences very well.	Awesome for consumer-facing teams. Unfortunately, not granular or actionable enough for most IT teams.	Doesn't get specific enough about what the obstacles are or why they exist. Only measures one thing: effort.	Fine-tuned for excellence and specifically for badass, best-in-industry service orgs; companies who are happy being "good" are unlikely to see the same value or returns.

CSAT: This is what 99 percent of IT departments use. That alone should be enough reason to disqualify it as a transformational tool. This is an email or pop-up that asks a customer if she was satisfied or not by an interaction. Your CSAT score is the percentage of people who were "satisfied." It typically only collects feedback from people who have recently worked with IT.

NPS®, or Net Promoter Score®, is a simple, one-question survey: How likely are you to recommend us to a friend? It's used by such kings of customer satisfaction as the Ritz Carlton, Audi, Zappos, and Apple. Your NPS gets dinged if your customers are less than amazed and in love with your service. This is geared to engender world-class customer satisfaction for companies whose bottom lines depend on being the best.

CES, or Customer Effort Score™, is meant to work alongside NPS or CSAT surveys. The philosophy is interesting, but the general feedback is that it is death by survey to employ a second tool to add the context missing from your original survey.

QSTAC™ is referred to as the "golden metric" for an exclusive group of IT teams, mostly at tech companies. The QSTAC is the only survey with a 100 percent success rate at drastically improving customer satisfaction for IT support teams. It measures how the entire company feels about IT, not just those who've recently gone to IT for help. Full disclosure: I invented this, so I'm a bit biased, but I hope the track record speaks for itself!

If you have more money than time, pull out the checkbook, and QSTAC LLC can do all the work for you. If you have more time than money, the principles of the survey are open-sourced, and you can make a DIY survey that will blow doors off anything you've ever used. It's not hard; we'll cover how to make your own survey for free later. Also, if you're a nonprofit or a company making positive changes in the world, QSTAC does pro bono work every year as a way of paying it forward. Let us know!

DEEP DIVE: WHY THE C.S.A.T. IS C.R.A.P.

As you can see in the chart above, IT departments can choose from a number of different surveys to get customer feedback. The worst of the bunch—sadly, but not surprisingly—is the one most often used by IT departments: the CSAT. The CSAT is fine if your goal is to not be hated. If you think providing "good" service meets your standards of excellence, by all means, go for it. If you want to be a badass team, however, just asking people if they're satisfied or not has never resulted in Badass IT Support. A huge internet company I worked for once called me into a meeting and basically mic-dropped after showing me its historical CSAT scores. A near-perfect 99 percent

CSAT score for eight consecutive quarters. This felt a little incongruous since they were paying me six figures to fix their customer perception, but whatevs. Money is money.

The first QSTAC survey we sent out at that company came back with far from perfect scores—twenty percentage points below other companies I had worked with. When we presented these scores to the managers, you could have heard a pin drop. Then the excuses started to fly. One guy's complaint spoke volumes and perfectly illustrated the difference between the two surveys:

"Brennan, this QSTAC score is imbalanced. You get way more points for 'Awesome!' responses than you do for 'good' ones."

"Exactly," I said.

"Oh," he said.

Yeah, oh.

"AMAZING!" IS THE NEW "GOOD"

Listen, I don't want to shit all over the survey you use—that's not my intention. The CSAT is the only survey most people know about, and it's a widely recognized industry standard.

What I want to share with you is how an exclusive but growing number of companies now use a better-researched, NPS-inspired survey to transform their orgs into armies of badass IT professionals. You don't have to use the QSTAC; you can even make your own, which I'll cover at the end of this chapter. The point is, you can't use the same underwhelming tools if you want to become an industry leader. Again, garbage in, garbage out.

When you measure success with CSAT, you only learn how many people are satisfied and how many are not. Sure, it gives you a nice graph to show upper management. But in my experience, the data doesn't transform your operation. Most of your customers are "satisfied," and that's the extent of your insight. When you go to the best restaurant in New York City, you don't say, "Wow, I was satisfied with that caviar-encrusted Wagyu filet mignon." You say, "Dude, that steak was the bomb!" You don't hear people say, "Wow, you have to go see *Hamilton*. I was satisfied with the performance!" You won't catch someone who loves driving saying, "Wow, this Audi handles so satisfactorily."

Not differentiating between amazing and pretty good sets the bar way too low. You don't get to badass by *satisfying* your customers—you get there by blowing their minds. Inevitably, mediocre teams flaunt their 99 percent positive responses as the pinnacle of IT support. I've seen way too many underwhelming IT teams with 99 percent CSAT scores to believe this is accurate. If it were, I'd be working at Starbucks in Berkeley instead of flying all over the world consulting for Fortune 500 companies.

"Amazing!" is the new "good."

NET PROMOTER SCORE (NPS): ALMOST PERFECT

NPS is the gold standard for most consumer industries. Apple, Amazon, the Ritz Carlton, and many other customer-service-oriented companies have used it to make sure they give the most badass service possible. These companies know the NPS delivers hyper loyal customers and a better bottom line. Although a few companies, like IBM for one, have used this with great success for IT support teams; it tends not to be granular enough for real transformation in IT. That said, it's worth learning about in case you can find a way to use it for your company.

The NPS method is simple but vicious. It's based on a single question: How likely are you to recommend us to a friend? NPS is measured on a ten-point scale, and when I say it's vicious, I mean any score below a nine is seen as a failure. Not only that, but the ten is on the far right side of the page, which means you have to skip over eight other numbers before you get to nine or ten. Love it!

People who take the NPS survey are put into one of three categories depending on their response: If you give a nine or a ten, you're a promoter. If you give a seven or eight, you're passive. Six or below, you're a detractor. This type of survey recognizes the power of word-of-mouth advertising. The more nines and tens you get, the more customers are likely to sing your praises to other potential customers. That's the most effective marketing you can do.

NPS is not designed for internal IT teams, however. It doesn't make sense to ask an employee, "Would you recommend IT to a coworker?" They're the only IT department at the company, so the premise doesn't apply. To transform into a badass IT org, you need to know specifically what to fix, not just how much folks like you, and that requires another level or two of granularity.

THE QSTAC METHOD: A DIFFERENT KIND OF SURVEY

Most CIOs and IT managers look at survey results with skepticism. I'm an IT director at a Fortune 500 company, and I certainly do! We've all tried surveys, and none has resulted in an IT department that kills it at every turn. Consultants come and go, and all leave behind these sparkling surveys that don't reveal anything or improve these IT departments. What's more, these surveys don't leave CIOs and IT managers with meaningful data. What areas do they need to improve on first? What kind of score reveals a significant change in their IT department? How do you know when you've won?

We wanted a survey that would accurately measure our customers' perception of our team's performance and give us specific feedback on how to improve. We also wanted it to be as scientific as possible.

Enter QSTAC, the survey made for badass IT folks by badass IT folks. Our core team brought their experiences from PayPal, Twitter, Jawbone, Box, 21st Century Fox, Red Bull, and Pivotal Labs and designed what I think is the NPS of IT surveys. It's been 100 percent successful so far, so, please, don't be the first to fuck that up! :)

Motivated to find a better way than CSAT surveys to accurately measure customer sentiment, I threw myself into research, cracking open my old statistics textbooks and studying the latest research on surveys. I bought a membership to the Help Desk Institute (HDI) and downloaded every white paper and research report I found. It became a passion project that ate up months of my life. Luckily, I was single at the time.

What I learned was that with surveys, simpler is better. Your survey must be quick and easy and only ask about things you'll act upon. If it takes more than sixty seconds to complete, you're toast. Your questions must be clear and distinct, so respondents aren't confused about what you ask. For example, don't ask about both "speed" and "responsiveness," because customers might confuse the two, and your results will be misleading. We started out with the thirty most common areas of excellence that the industry measures, and then pared it down till we had five: **Q**uality, **S**peed, **T**echnical Knowledge, **A**pproachability, and **C**ommunication: **QSTAC**.

I was prepared to refine those five questions, depending on how customers interpreted them, but after four years of using the survey, those five questions have stuck. This tells me we got it right from the start.

I also wanted to be respectful of people's time and the cost to the company. If there are ten thousand employees and the survey takes ten minutes to complete, that costs the company a metric shit ton in lost productivity. The QSTAC takes less than sixty seconds to score us on all five dimensions and gives us incredibly actionable open-ended feedback about what we do well and what we could do better. Simple as that. Boom, boom, boom.

None of the survey questions are mandatory because that can cause people to bail out and not finish the survey. We make it as easy as possible, and we bribe the hell out of people to take it each quarter by holding prize drawings with fancy prizes like Apple watches, VR headsets, and iPads. It's the least we can do for taking up sixty seconds of their time, and it's also super dope to walk up to someone's desk with an Apple watch and say. "Hey, you won! Thanks for taking the survey!"

MAKING YOUR OWN SURVEY: A DIY GUIDE

Are you underwhelmed by CSAT, too, but not feeling the QSTAC? With a little research, you can create your own survey that's ten times more actionable and transformational than old-school methods. For those DIY folks out there, here are some tips I learned from years of experience and months of research that will help you in your quest to create a badass survey.

Reliability: If your data isn't reliable, you're wasting everyone's time. One cool hack for this at bigger companies is to compare random samples of 20 percent and 50 percent of your responses to your total responses at the end. For instance, if you get ten thousand responses, your survey is pretty reliable if the first thousand responses and the first five thousand responses have about the same score as the final ten thousand. This means your survey reliably measures the overall sentiment. The QSTAC tool we use shows real-time responses and scores as they come in, so after the first thousand scores, we typically know what ballpark the rest of our scores will be in, even though thousands of people have yet to respond.

Accuracy: Accuracy is how close your results are to reality, how your customers truly feel in real life. In other words, if your Omaha office improves, their score should go up accordingly. If anecdotally the sentiment is worse this quarter, your scores should generally reflect that sentiment as well. Traditional CSAT surveys don't accurately paint a picture of overall customer sentiment. Avoid this common mistake: CSAT surveys often only poll folks who have interacted with IT in a given period. A lot of the smartest people I know enthusiastically *avoid* IT at all costs because they don't want some random IT guy fooling around with their phone or computer. In these cases, their appraisal is never recorded in CSAT because they've never officially gotten help. But QSTAC goes out to everyone in the company, regardless of whether you called IT for help, so you get richer data. The most eye-opening data in my experience is from these people who will never interact with IT if they don't have to. These tend to be the thought leaders at your company, so missing out on their feedback will never get you where you need to go.

Here are a few other helpful takeaways:

⏻ Start with anonymous surveys. QSTAC is anonymous, so employees giving low scores don't worry about resentment or retaliation from IT. This also improves the response rate.

- ⏻ Focus on getting honest responses. When we send the email announcing our survey, we always use these exact words: "Be brutally honest; we can take it!" We want people to know that we are serious about hearing their criticisms. Some surveys are sent out with a wink that suggests you only want good feedback. We try to use language that conveys that we are more interested in honesty.

- ⏻ Let people know that their feedback will actually make a difference. The results are more accurate when you explain *why* you conduct the survey and how you plan to use the feedback to improve.

- ⏻ At first, most people won't believe that you'll listen to their criticism. Don't worry. But by the second or third survey, your customers will have noticed that you *are*, in fact, listening—and addressing their concerns. In later surveys, when you ask what you can do better, you start to see responses like, "You've already done it! Thanks for fixing X last quarter—you guys rock!"

- ⏻ Word your email carefully. We agonize over the wording every quarter because we want to convey an intentional vibe and style. We want to come across as likable. Even the wording of the email you send out the survey with is an opportunity to transform your relationship with your customers.

- ⏻ Keep the email short! It's good office etiquette, and it shows people that you value their time. Most people, if they see a long email that's not mandatory, will delete it without opening it. We always edit down our emails, having learned that every word we cut from the email announcement means a dozen more people will take the survey.

⏻ Bribery gets you everywhere. In the subject line of the email, we emphasize that it's a sixty-second survey and that there are awesome prizes. I have no idea why, but when you offer a prize drawing at work, people go berserk. I personally could care less about a new Apple watch or an iPad, but people absolutely lose their minds when they win something like that at the office. Prizes are the key to getting a 35 percent response rate. It's not a fail if you get less, but 35 percent is the magic number that I've found ensures accuracy. Shoot for this response rate and keep the survey open until you're at least close.

To summarize: Keep your survey short and actionable, explain *why* you're sending it and what you'll use the data for, and then shamelessly bribe the hell out of your customers to get a 35 percent response rate. You got this, girl!

FROM BASELINE TO GOAL LINE

If you aspire to be badass, to reluctantly quote Vanilla Ice, anything less than the best is a felony. I *really* hope my editor takes that line out.

The feedback from the first QSTAC or other well-built survey you send out is always a hard pill to swallow. For everyone. Make sure there are no guns or pills around when you dive into the responses. You will probably learn that your IT team is not as good as you thought they were. This is normal, but it still stings. Also, it is absolutely maddening for us as IT professionals to read anonymous complaints and not know the context or who had these experiences. It's rough, but it's the first step toward improvement.

The first survey gives you your baseline scores, and the more the feedback stings, the more actionable the data is. That's good because you come away with clear-cut ideas about what your team needs to work on. Now you know what truly matters to your customers. As a result, you know exactly how and where to improve.

This honest feedback from customers results in a much more effective strategy than a bunch of IT managers sitting around a table building a roadmap based on their instincts or hunches. With the survey results in, you can now build a data-driven strategy. Since you used a research-based, reliable, and accurate survey, you know your data is good and that you're guaranteed to get a higher rating next time if you act on even some of that feedback.

MEASURING SUCCESS: THE SECOND SURVEY AND BEYOND

Now we're getting somewhere! You have your baseline. You have actionable data from your customers. You take action on that data and spend a quarter letting that data shape your customer experience. Shit, it's Q2 already? Time to see how you did! Remember, no firearms or pills in close proximity when you read the results, just in case.

You send out the second survey and then head to the bar and wait. The suspense will kill you, so a stiff drink always helps. While surveys don't need to give real-time updates, since they're only open a week or two, we added real-time reporting to the QSTAC mobile experience, because we were always too eager to wait for all the responses to come in. Trust me; after hitting *send* on a survey going out to thousands of employees, whether you're the CIO or an intern, you're going to sit there refreshing your browser for the next hour or two in anticipation of what your customers had to say.

I have my own ritual for survey day; feel free to adopt it. I hit *send* and stare at the dashboard to make sure responses come in cleanly. They start pouring in within about sixty seconds. Then I make a Sazerac or a Manhattan or something equally pretentious, light up a cigar, and stare at the results as they come in from all over the world. The whole day is brutal. We usually send it out in the morning on the East Coast and then watch on pins and needles as Omaha, California, Asia, and Europe wake up in turn and take the survey. It's maddening, but the excitement you get when you crush last quarter's scores is amazeballs.

Then it's done. You take a look at the damage. Whoa, London is up twenty points! Glad we fixed that printing issue there. What the hell happened in Rio? That manager has to go. New York beat San Francisco again—that's three quarters in a row. The West Coast guys are gonna get so competitive next quarter over this.

And so on. After the second survey comes back, you have a new superpower: knowing precisely which of your initiatives elicited change and which fell flat.

The results, even several quarters in, can still be surprising. I remember one particularly humbling example at one company. We had a two-hundred-person office in Middle America that was chock-full of nerdy, hyperintelligent engineers. These were the smartest guys in the room and very hard to please. We wanted to help bump up their scores, so my VP and I flew down to their office in person to show some love and watch them work in their element. We did a flashy presentation for the whole office and couldn't wait to see their scores the next quarter. We nailed it, or so we thought. Then the next quarter's results came in.

WTF? Normally a team will improve after an executive visit, especially by me, right? So I thought. In fact, the scores actually went *down* after we went there. We were a total flop! Ouch.

When we shared this with our team, a twenty-two-year-old boy genius from Upstate New York said, "Hey, I'm happy to go down there next quarter."

Go for it, man. Good luck. Obviously, our fancy executive visit was not what these engineers considered badass.

He went down there and was able to talk on their level and solve complex networking and computing issues that I couldn't even pronounce. Since then, QSTAC scores at that engineering office have shot through the roof and remain at best-in-industry levels. We send him there once or twice a quarter now to keep doing whatever it is he's doing that people there love so much. The experience was humbling for me, but a little humble pie tastes awesome when a frustrated office gets blown away by your team. Score one for Badass IT Support and nerdy boy geniuses from Upstate New York.

Regardless of which survey you use, letting your customers set your strategy and judge your success shifts the balance of power to *them*. This is what being customer-centric is about. No one cares if *we* think we are awesome. It's when *our customers* say we're awesome that it becomes true. If you take away nothing else from this book, remember this: Use a data-driven strategy-based 100 percent on honest feedback from your customers, and you'll get closer to badass every quarter. And your people will love you for it.

THE QSTAC METHOD: REAL-LIFE SUCCESS STORIES

These stories are based on feedback I got from the QSTAC survey, but they could apply to any customer feedback from any survey. It's all about being responsive.

Giving your customers a voice is worthwhile if you act on what they tell you. Here are a few examples of how we responded to feedback with simple changes that had a big impact. Always remember, the best ideas don't come from people who provide the service; they come from the people who *experience* the service.

THE IT GREMLINS

Remember Dom, the "go fuck yourself" guy from the Introduction? Dom's attitude was a symptom of a systemic problem. The first QSTAC survey at that company ranked the whole team as low on approachability. It was shocking to me because they were all nice, fun people, but when I looked at the open-ended feedback, an easy fix was obvious.

Customers visiting the IT area found everyone wearing headphones and acting put out when a customer asked for something. The marketing team confided in me that they called the techs "IT gremlins" because they were so grumpy when you asked for help. In truth, the techs were often simply busy on projects that required focus, and as such weren't as accommodating as they needed to be to wow our customers.

In these situations, we look for a solution that helps both sides. How do we give our technicians time and space to do project work and still have a welcoming, approachable help desk?

The win-win, in this case, was commandeering a lounge area, putting up a TV and a few white standing desks, and hanging a sign that said, "IT Support." We established a schedule for the techs; when it was your turn at the help desk, you couldn't wear headphones or do project work. When they were at the help desk, their job was to hang out, play music, keep hilarious GIFs looping on the big TV screen, and greet people passing by.

This is a common, uber-simple solution, but this team had just never gotten around to adopting it. When I suggested it initially, the team invoked that famous IT catchphrase, "We've tried that before. It didn't work." Luckily, I was the boss, so I said, "Well, we're going to try it again and do it better this time." Not surprisingly, the next round of scores rocketed up, and customers were thrilled. From IT gremlins to rock stars with two standing desks and a TV. Done!

GETTING UP TO SPEED

I mentioned earlier that when I first got to Yahoo!, you couldn't email IT. Chat wait times were averaging thirty minutes or more. Not what anyone would call badass. Even after we opened an email channel, we still needed to shorten wait times for phone and chat support if we were going to blow our customers' minds.

I told leadership that I could get it down from thirty minutes to thirty seconds. My VP, always eager to one-up me, said, "No way, dude! It should be five seconds!" Thanks, boss.

I actually love working with her because of that attitude; she always ups my game. I agreed to set our goal at five-second wait times, and then dove into the data to figure out how the hell we would get there. We shared the goal with our team and started tracking wait times, sharing those metrics with the team as well. After a few weekly reports, the weirdest thing happened: chat wait times just went down. On their own! It seemed like magic, but the real change agent was much simpler. Our team was filled with smart, competitive nerds with creativity and crazy work ethics. Their competitiveness against the defined goal resulted in their finding smarter ways to work and organize themselves until five seconds became the average wait time worldwide. The data itself transformed the team. It turns out that when you give good data and a clear goal to smart, competitive people, they find a way to make it happen.

I should mention that it wasn't as if the techs weren't working hard before; it's just that no one had ever asked them to do more. No one had ever set the expectations any higher. Our QSTAC score on the speed dimension shot up the next quarter to record levels, and I was flooded with emails from other leaders about how much better phone and chat support was.

It's amazing what happens when you raise the bar. I would see this happen time and time again; when you set higher expectations and monitor progress toward achieving those expectations, people respond. More importantly, they enjoy their jobs more, feel satisfied, and look for even more ways to get better.

GETTING CREATIVE

Being badass often means doing things that are outside your job description.

At Twitter, we decided we needed to fix the company's problems with videoconferencing. The company was using four different types of videoconferencing, and it was not only confusing to manage, but it was costing the company a fortune unnecessarily. We had to put everyone on the same system to stop hemorrhaging money. The vendor we chose to use was called Blue Jeans Video.

We knew from our survey that a lot of our customers would be unhappy when we took away the videoconferencing system they were used to. However, if everyone didn't adopt it right away, it would be disruptive to the whole company, so we took a soft approach to manage the customer's perception of this new service.

Instead of just rolling out a new system, I dusted off my director's hat and made a video. I had produced a short film in grad school and had the video chops, but I was going to need some help to make this a success and not an embarrassing waste of resources.

For starters, I recruited the coolest influencers and culture leaders from the company to help me out. We filmed the head of internal communications doing yoga while joining on a videoconference on her phone. We had another exec do a video conference on his bike. We wanted to show people how cool the system was by showing some of our company's thought leaders enjoying its flexibility. We made it funny, cool, and sold it hard! I probably spent twenty hours just editing that fucking three-minute video!

We played the video at an all-hands meeting with the whole company, and it was a great success. We knew ahead of time that switching systems would be a headache, but we had empathy for our customers and explained how this system would help them in a way that they would pay attention to. Sending out an email no one would read was not going to get everyone on board. We showed them how cool the platform was, and most importantly, we had influential people who weren't from IT endorsing the new system. For you entrepreneurs out there, this is called "social proof." We reframed the change as a fun thing rather than an annoyance, and moved the entire company over in record time, saving the company a boatload of money.

Again, your success depends on wowing your customers. My CIO and VP love me because they get emails every week from people in the company telling them they have the best IT team they've ever seen in their entire career. This kind of customer enthusiasm doesn't come from processes and procedures. You'll only get there by being creative and thinking outside of the box.

Feeling creative? Feeling ready? Of course, you are, you badass, you! We're in the home stretch. Let's do this. On to my favorite section of the book, Part Four.

THE REAL SHIT: TRANSFORMING YOUR TEAM INTO A BADASS SUPPORT ORGANIZATION

THE EASY PART: WRITING A BADASS STRATEGY

Victorious warriors win first and then go to war, while defeated warriors go to war first and then seek to win.

—SUN TZU, *THE ART OF WAR*

The team we built from scratch at Jawbone was by all accounts the most Badass IT Support team ever assembled. No one had ever seen anything like it. I still haven't been able to re-create it at other companies.

This team wasn't assembled accidentally. It came about through a rare confluence of opportunity, talent, and timing. We had the opportunity to build a team from the ground up, which is a rare circumstance for many companies, and we designed a team to meet the specific needs of an atypical start-up. On top of that, we had managers who trusted us and were willing to let us assemble the team we felt we needed. We made the most of the opportunity.

We established dozens of unconventional rules for that team. One of them, as you may recall from Chapter One, was, "Don't bring your dick to the office." Another, and perhaps equally unconventional directive was that everyone had to read *The Art of War* and carry it around with them at all times in case we needed it. This rule was no joke. If you were in a meeting and couldn't produce your copy of the book, that shit was going on your performance review. Period.

Why? First, we thought it was hilarious, and it made our executives laugh every time. Second, it lent an air of mystery to our IT Team. When employees saw one of our IT girls or guys on an office couch reading *The Art of War* during lunch, they couldn't help but wonder why. Most importantly, however, we really did believe this 2,500-year-old text helped teach our techs to solve problems on their own.

This book is filled with war strategies that can be applied to your work or business. For example, Sun Tzu understood the value of foreknowledge. Those who study the enemy and the terrain and use that wisdom in battle are more likely to win. This helped our IT guys and girls understand the value of sharing information and analyzing problems before tackling them. When Sun Tzu said, "He will win whose army is animated by the same spirit throughout all its ranks," we believed him and followed suit. We knew that attempting any endeavor without having a thought-out strategy jeopardized our success as a badass team.

I've never dictated that any other IT team of mine carry around that book since. But Jawbone was a special group of crazy-ass artists, and the discipline and philosophy described in that book resonated with the team and pulled us together as a badass unit. When your IT team reaches a certain level of peak performance, unconventional things like mandating Sun Tzu just start making sense. But to get there, you must first lay out your team's strategy to become a badass army of IT professionals.

Don't worry; this is the easy part.

In Part Three of this book, we stayed high-level. We gave your customers a voice and used that voice to make changes that met their needs. However, philosophy class is over. We've had enough theory. It's time now for the nuts and bolts. Time for the real shit.

Part Four is a step-by-step guide to implementing Badass IT Support at your company. In this chapter, we'll punch up your data-driven strategy to make sure it kicks ass in real life.

We'll tackle the hard part in Chapter Eight, which is about mastering firing, hiring, and culture. Finally, we'll end with the fun stuff in Chapter Nine, which is about winning, building dope shit and paying it forward. These sections will be a straightforward how-to guide to becoming a badass IT org in real life.

Ready? Let's do this.

STRATEGY FOR BADASSES

So, one might ask, if the strategy writes itself, why do we need a whole chapter on it? Great question. It's true that if you have a tool like QSTAC, the data from your customers will dictate your strategy. However, given the importance of strategy to your success, you must fine-tune it and execute it like a boss. In other words, you need a strategy for rolling out your strategy. Very meta, right? This chapter will help you punch up your data-driven strategy and even give you some freebies we've learned from other badass teams. It'll be simple and short. Let's do it.

SHOCK AND AWE

Time your QSTAC survey so it goes out near the end of

each quarter, right before you start planning. This way your strategy for the next quarter is pulled from the freshest data. Since your data is accurate and current, the problems are clear, and you can see how to fix them with style. I've found that all customer feedback falls into two categories: easy fixes (the low-hanging fruit) and complex changes that take weeks or months to implement. So, how does a Badass IT Support team tackle these two categories?

Shock and awe, baby!

The shock-and-awe strategy jumpstarts your customer-centric, badass org. Shock them with some quick victories. Awe them with lasting, systemic changes that build long-term trust and esteem for your team.

Nothing shocks customers more than when you solve problems they identified just a week before. No one expects that from IT. The bar has been so low for so long that your customers will be blown away by that level of responsiveness.

The awe comes later when lasting improvements start to affect their day-to-day lives, making them more productive. First, they say, "Wow! They listened! I'm shocked!" Then, over time, you start to hear, "Oh, yeah! Videoconferencing works every day! These guys aren't just talk; they're for real!"

LOW-HANGING FRUIT

Finding easy-to-fix, low-hanging fruit is critical to getting this shock-and-awe strategy started. Need some ideas to prime the pump? Here are some freebies that we call "easy rockers," a term we borrowed from the Wilco documentary, *I Am Trying to Break Your Heart*. Easy rockers are simple things you can implement quickly that are guaranteed to please your customers. In other words, they give you a lot of bang for your buck.

Easy Rocker 1: Pump Up the Jams

If you have a walk-up IT area, buy a Spotify account and a big-ass wireless speaker and crank up some tunes. Creating a party vibe in the walk-up area is a great way to "brand" your team as a fun crew, and it will set the stage for more natural, positive interactions.

Easy Rocker 2: Say Hello

I've mentioned this before, but it bears repeating: greet your customers enthusiastically the second they walk into your IT area. Don't wait until they reach the counter. Even the friendliest techs can get tunnel vision when working on a problem and neglect to immediately greet new customers when they walk in. Break that habit.

Your techs feel at home in the IT area. However, your customers only go there occasionally and need to be assured that they are welcomed and important—particularly since many customers over the years have grown accustomed to being ignored or demeaned by IT workers. Take the time to train your folks how to enthusiastically greet people. Practice. In our trainings, techs practiced saying things like, "Hi, Bill! Nice to see you. I'll be with you in just a few minutes when I'm done helping this customer." It sounds basic, but focusing on greetings will be a game changer that will cause your customers to take notice.

Easy Rocker 3: SCAN Your Tickets

I hate tickets. I hate looking at them. I hate reading through them. I hate that they exist.

Unfortunately, they're how most IT departments manage customer requests. But can a busy IT support worker who cranks out twenty to thirty tickets a day communicate thoroughly and accurately every time? Can an IT manager ensure that everyone is communicating clearly on each ticket? If there's an emergency, can you pull up a ticket and instantly know the status, history, and next steps?

The answer to all these questions is "yes."

To make ticket comments accessible, clear, and less annoying to everyone involved, I created the SCAN system for providing updates. SCAN stands for **S**tatus, **C**urrent plan, and **A**ction **N**eeded. Every time a tech updates a ticket, she uses a text expander with the three SCAN prompts. After Status, she writes what's happening, such as "Laptop has been shipped." For Current plan, she writes something like, "Laptop to arrive in Seattle on 10/14." In the Action Needed prompt, she writes down what needs to happen next and who'll be doing that task, such as "Local IT will inform Steve when his laptop is ready to pick up at the Seattle office."

Before the SCAN system, our customers would receive inconsistent or incomplete messages that annoyed or confused them. Techs are smart and well-meaning, but they aren't professional writers. Customers would read these hastily written comments and pull their hair out trying to figure out what they meant. With SCAN, every comment or email response is direct, clear, and easy to write—particularly after we automated the prompts with text expander. This system generates an informative and conversational email. It provides the specifics a customer needs to know. It also provides a clear trail of information for anyone in IT who needs to know what's happening with a particular ticket. Like it? Feel free to steal it!

Easy Rocker 4: Make It Rain

It's not enough to offer your coworkers cool prizes to take

the QSTAC survey. You also need to make a big deal about delivering those prizes to the lucky winners.

Nothing delights a customer more than having the whole IT team come up to her desk and present her with a new Apple watch or iPad Pro. This blows people away and makes them feel special, which everyone loves. Every quarter, I personally reach out to the winners of our QSTAC prize drawing, and the most common reaction I get is, "Wow, I didn't know anyone actually won those things!" Well, they do. And when you make a big deal out of that fact, word gets out, and even more people take the survey next time. This is the lowest-hanging fruit, and plus, it's always fun to make it rain fancy consumer electronics on the employees you serve.

MAKING SHIT UP

Okay, so what if your DIY survey wasn't designed well and comes back without much actionable data? Or, what if you're so damn productive that you've already finished your shock-and-awe campaign and executed all of your ideas? Don't worry. The coolest innovations take shape when you think you're out of ideas. Time to get inspired.

Look at the world around you and notice what's awesome in it. Then ask yourself, "How can I bring that to IT?" This is where great design comes from. Think about the iPhone design. Little icons with rounded corners wiggle around excitedly when you rearrange your home screen as if waiting to be picked up and taken for a ride. You might not remember it, but back then, that was some weird-ass shit to see on your phone!

Look around at what innovative companies in other industries do. Steve Jobs once said, "Good artists copy; great artists steal" (a line that Jobs himself attributed to Pablo Picasso). Whatever the case, think of companies in other industries that provide badass customer experiences, and use those proven methods to wow your own customers.

Here are a few ideas I'm working on at the moment. Do any inspire you?

- ⏻ A dope, professionally designed IT support app that lets customers do everything they need to do—search the knowledge base, live chat, or click-to-dial to connect with IT—from their phone or other mobile devices.
- ⏻ Chatbots that instantly answer common questions and get smarter with each one.
- ⏻ Voice-activated everything. Use a voice command to start a video conference or book a meeting. I can't wait for this one.
- ⏻ FedEx-like tracking numbers. You click on the number and see the status of your request anytime from any device.

⏻ Push notifications. These are so much more effective and friendly than email. Your phone buzzes, and you look at the locked screen. "Oh, sweet, my computer is fixed. Awesome!"

HAVE FUN WITH IT!

If this book resonates with you even a little, you're a badass at heart. I've included a lot of easy rockers and examples of things that our teams have done. But the most lasting impact you'll have will come from working with your team to develop your own customer-tailored ideas.

I hope this book gives you the incentive to shake off old-school IT expectations and follow your own inspiration. Have some fun! Make shit up. A strategy that comes from the heart will scale more for your team than anything you read in a book. I hope the stories and examples inspire you to think big and create your own magic. There is no greater bonding experience than to come up with an idea as a team and see it through to completion. When you go through that together, it has a lasting impact on everyone involved.

One afternoon a few years back, I had just hopped off the train at the Caltrain station on Townsend Street in San Francisco and was headed toward a friend's bar for happy hour. Suddenly, I heard someone yell, "Whattup Brennan!"

I spun around and here comes Julian, the bearded hipster I'd hired and trained at Jawbone—the one an executive nicknamed "Junior Awesome." I hadn't seen him in over a year. He pulled up to me on his fixed-gear bike, doing that cool skid stop that bearded, fixie-riding hipsters do.

He was in a hurry, but he took the time to reach into his Chrome messenger bag and pulled out a copy of *The Art of War*. Fuck yeah! He smiled widely and rode off to wherever the hell bearded hipsters go on their fixed-gear bikes.

The fact that Julian still carried *The Art of War* in his bag a year after I'd left Jawbone reminded me that leaders can have a lasting impact on their employees' lives. When you work on a badass team, that experience becomes the new gold standard for how awesome a team can be. Every team you work on from then on will be compared to that one beautiful moment in time when you were the best in the world at something. That is an experience no one ever forgets.

THE HARD PART: FIRING, HIRING, AND MANAGING CULTURE

There is no rule book for firing, hiring, and culture. I'm not an expert on any of them, but I can give you a framework that might help in your situation.

In this chapter, we'll cover a flowchart of who, when, how, and why to fire employees. For hiring, I'll give you a simple list of dos and don'ts. For culture, I'll give you examples of what has worked for me and let you develop a culture that works for your company.

Layoffs. Underperforming employees. Resumes and interview panels. There's a reason this chapter isn't called the fun part. This is the hard part, but it's also the important part; firing, hiring, and culture will make or break your team. It's what separates good teams from badass ones. Firing and hiring the right people and managing a kick-ass team culture are essential to becoming the best in the industry.

Ready? Let's do this.

FIRING

Firing people sucks. Managers often feel like they failed, either by hiring the wrong person, putting them in the wrong job, or not training them properly. Some managers deserve to feel bad, but many others don't.

The fired employee feels like a failure too. They often leave the company with hard feelings. I can relate. I've been in the workforce for twenty-five years, but I got fired once, and I will never forget the twerpy, twenty-something manager who let me go. I wouldn't normally remember someone like that, but because he fired me, his image is burned in my mind, and I would gleefully punch him in the face the next time I saw him.

Firing—whether you're getting it or giving it—is fucking emotional.

Leaders don't make emotional decisions. They make

badass decisions. You must set the emotions aside and make your decision based on what's best for your company, your team, and your employee. Since this can be a touchy topic, we'll simplify the discussion and cover the who, when, why, and how to fire employees. There's even a chart for you visual types.

FIRING TOXIC EMPLOYEES: WHO, WHEN, WHY, AND HOW

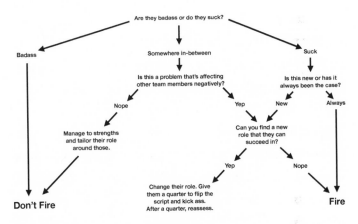

Who should you fire? Attitude is everything. You will never regret firing someone who has a bad or negative attitude, or who complains frequently but never offers any solutions. Think about your employees whose attitudes bring everyone else down. Now imagine never having to work with them again. If this excites you, it's time for them to update their LinkedIn and begin an extended vacation far away from your company and most importantly your team.

When should you fire these people? If you have someone with a toxic attitude on your team, put down this book, call HR, and start the firing process right now. However, if someone has a great attitude but has developed performance problems, there's still hope. Think about moving them to a job better suited to their talents. Don't fire a good employee because you have them in the wrong job. Find them a job that inspires them.

Why is it important to fire toxic employees right away? There are many reasons. They tank productive discussions. They steal time and headspace from you. And, most importantly, their negativity is contagious. I've had to lay off many people in recent years, but for each toxic employee I've let go, my only regret is not doing it sooner. Your team's morale skyrockets when toxic employees are fired. Firing a Negative Nancy or a Mopey Moe inspires your team better than any slide deck or motivational speech. Your team will love you and respect you as a leader.

How should you fire someone? I don't believe in performance improvement plans (PIPs); they take weeks, and they typically prolong the inevitable. Many employees use that time to find a new job, but when they don't, you must let them go. Be direct and honest. Slide them as big a severance check as possible so they can take care of their families. Have them sign an even bigger nondisclosure agreement and be done with it. Even if they were dingleberries at work, it's important to give them a strong severance package. You'll feel better about yourself. Generous severance packages also help your reputation; word about how you treat people when they're laid off spreads through the industry, and if you're fair and honest, you'll get better job applicants in the future.

Finally, show some empathy. Firing is a serious, profound event—for you and the employee. Managers are partially to blame when an employee fails. They didn't hire the right person, they didn't train them well, or they weren't creative enough to find the employees' true strengths. The employee may be a bad person and may have fucked up, but at least part of that is on you.

Managers should never take firing lightly or turn to it too quickly. Remember, you might get fired someday yourself. If that were to happen, how would you like to be treated? Would you like to be given a chance to succeed in another job at that company? Or take a cut in pay or a lower-level position? As managers, we must understand that even poor-performing employees have rent, families, and kids' braces to pay for. This is their livelihood.

This is about being a good human to another human, so give your poorly performing employees time to find another job, even if you stick them in the East Bumfuck office for a few months. Is there anything you can do to make it easier on their life? If so, do it. Human beings are lucky to be the evolved race on Earth, so be good to each other before the aliens come and enslave us all.

HIRING

Everyone thinks they are a good judge of character, but few of us are. As a psychotherapist, I clocked over five thousand hours talking to people about themselves, and I still feel I have a ton to learn about hiring the right folks.

The standard hiring process of a phone interview, a couple of face-to-face interviews, and reference checks is an outdated and laughably inadequate way to decide whether to hire someone. Still, everyone uses it. You probably use it. I use it.

However, hiring great people is not a science. Finding and hiring great people is an art that starts with mastering a few basic techniques.

BADASS HIRING DON'TS

- ⏻ Never hire because you need bodies to manage the workload. An understaffed badass team is ten times better than a fully staffed team with a couple of weak links.
- ⏻ Never hire anyone you're not stoked about. There are

a lot of incredible people out there. If your recruiters aren't finding them, buy a LinkedIn premium account and find them yourself.

⏻ Do not exclusively hire people who are just like you. You need people who look at common problems from different angles. Everyone learns in that environment. Diversity scales.

⏻ Never hire anyone who is even slightly creepy. If you have all dudes on your interview panel, have a socially intelligent woman interview the person as well. Follow up with anyone the candidate interacted with on the day of their interview. If the applicant killed the in-person interviews but made the receptionist uncomfortable by staring at her boobs, that is not someone you want on your team!

⏻ Never hire anyone with even a whiff of negativity. If they're negative in an interview, they have toxic employee written all over them.

⏻ Don't buy in to the computer science degree fallacy. Or any degree for that matter. Many well-meaning executives require that all candidates must come from a top ten school or have a computer science degree. Google did that until the data discredited the policy, and they dropped it. If your company requires credentials that don't lead to Badass IT Support, fight to be exempt from bullshit rules that keep you from hiring the perfect team.

BADASS HIRING DOS

- ⏻ Hire interesting, enthusiastic people who are special in some way. If someone isn't passionate about anything, how can they be passionate about IT support? If someone is the best in another area of life, they'll want to be the best at wowing your customers too. These are the people who make up Badass IT Support teams.

- ⏻ Hire as many women as men. The closer you come to a fifty-fifty balance of men and women, the easier it is to become badass. Most IT teams need a woman's touch!

- ⏻ Promote from within. If someone already is a great culture match for your company, hire them over someone from the outside.

- ⏻ Hire adaptable people. Shit changes, man. People who are stuck in their ways don't last on Badass IT Support teams.

- ⏻ Hire socially intelligent people. This is a hard one to suss out, but look for people who are fun to chat with and can carry on a conversation with a wide variety of people. Look for folks who are good listeners especially, as this makes others feel like they've made a good connection with them. Hiring fairs or company events are a great opportunity to see if your candidate is socially intelligent; they allow you to observe how they carry themselves outside of the interview room.

ABOUT CORE VALUES AND CULTURE

I used to think companies and IT departments needed core values. Core values are meant to give your team a shared language to discuss issues and filter all decisions.

However, core values alienate employees who don't believe in them. A team's core values should reflect the sentiments of all team members. Core values that well up from your team members should be the lens for examining every problem or decision.

When Twitter was small—just two hundred people or so—it developed ten core values, with bullet points like "get it right," "simplify," and "communicate fearlessly to build trust."

When the company grew from hundreds of employees to thousands, senior managers worried about how to maintain the company culture they loved in the face of tremendous growth. How could they maintain the company's guiding principles when scores of new hires came from companies like Google, Oracle, and Facebook, who all have their own culture?

Twitter's approach was ingenious. Company leaders sent out a questionnaire to every person in the company and asked them what they valued. The leaders boiled down the answers, and their company's core values emerged.

As the company quintupled in size over two years, those values remained a key part of Twitter's culture.

I was on the core values team at Twitter and taught an hour-long session on values to hundreds of employees on their first week at the company. But when I tried to implement core values the same way at other companies, the process felt contrived, and the values lost their potency over time. There was one exception: "A Truly Badass Customer Experience Is Always Priority Number One." This is the stickiest, most impactful value I've ever seen. If you think about implementing core values for your team, I highly recommend sticking with one, central value. Feel free to steal this one; it's an easy rocker.

MANAGING TO STRENGTHS

I declared 2017 "the year of managing to strengths" and made this my primary goal as a leader.

While it's wise to get rid of toxic employees, what do you do with an employee who is a great person but is no longer inspired by their job? Firing isn't the answer. Instead, focus on what they do well and try to create or find a position where they can excel.

At one company, we had an East Coast manager who ran a great team and had the best scores every quarter. The problem was he skipped "off-site" events—such as retreats where we might do some team building or talk about our life's passions. Many leaders value these sessions, but this guy didn't, and it angered those who felt he was slacking off by not participating.

I was in a tight spot. I didn't want to fire the guy. He did a great job; he just wasn't into the touchy-feely stuff. On the other hand, everyone else who was required to participate showed up, so how could we look the other way with this guy?

I asked myself, "Do we need him to go to talk about his feelings in order to have a strong, functioning team?" The answer was "no", so I reassigned him and asked him to focus on what he could excel at. We rewrote his job description, called his team "Special Ops," and no longer required him to attend touchy-feely sessions. We managed to his strengths rather than to his weaknesses. He became one of the best managers in his organization.

Rather than squeezing people into rigid roles that don't fit their strengths, find a role the person loves and does well. If you have a manager who is well-organized but doesn't like interacting with people, give him the detailed inventory work that he loves and everyone else hates. Take the guy who loves people out of the equipment room and put him with customers. Managing to strengths is a secret weapon. Once you implement it, you wonder how you ever did without it. Without a single call to HR, you can turn a problem employee into a badass employee.

SAY WHAT?

I consider myself an easygoing guy, but there are certain statements that Badass IT Support teams never utter, especially on one of my teams. Here are two phrases that will stop one of my meetings dead in their tracks if someone utters them.

"THAT'S NOT MY JOB."

Make sure your team knows that you never want to hear this. It is everyone's job to do anything it takes to ensure a badass customer experience. If you hear someone say, "That's not my job," you should reply, "you're right! With that attitude, your job is somewhere else—at another company."

"WE'VE TRIED THAT BEFORE, AND IT DIDN'T WORK."

That kind of defeatist attitude has no place on a Badass IT Support team. When I arrived at Box, I suggested we set up a dedicated, walk-up IT area staffed by the most skilled and friendliest technicians. The first thing I heard was,

"We tried that before. It didn't work." My first thought was, "Did it fail because you wanted it to fail?" But I didn't say that. Instead, I said, "Well, sometimes it takes a few tries before you get it right. Let's give it another shot, shall we?"

The "we tried it before" attitude blocks innovation and is lazy. If you miss a shot in basketball, you don't quit shooting and just pass the ball every time. No, you work on your shooting and get better at it. If it didn't work the first time, it might be because you didn't execute it right or the timing was wrong. That doesn't mean you shouldn't try it again.

That dedicated walkup IT area we created at box was a huge success. Our customers loved it, and our QSTAC scores went through the roof, even though they had tried the same thing before and not found success.

Train your team to call each other out every time someone starts to say, "We tried it before..." Let them have some fun with it. This will remind everyone to have a "make it happen" attitude, which in turn will—surprise!—result in your team making things happen with max badassishness.

Phew! OK, hard part over. I'm hopeful this helps you fire, hire, and manage your culture like the badass that you are.

We're on the home stretch, people! You're very close to

having all the tools you need to win and win big. You're destined for badass status. Take a break, grab a celebratory drink, smoke 'em if you got 'em. It's time for the fun part.

THE FUN PART: WINNING AND PAYING IT FORWARD

I love winning. It feels so damn good. We've all felt that way in one arena or another, but I can't wait for you to experience what it's like to transform your crew into an industry-leading, Badass IT Support team. It is a euphoric experience. Your team swells with pride knowing it's reached a summit that only a handful of IT support teams in the world have conquered.

It's especially satisfying because you set out to accomplish it of your own volition. You did it because it was the badass thing to do. After all of those obstacles and setbacks and nights and weekends of hard work, you won! There is nothing better than that first all-hands meeting where you release the survey scores that prove the team has achieved world-class status. You are in the 99.9th percentile of teams in the world. You are heads and shoulders above everyone else.

This achievement is significant because as an IT manager, you had to overcome IT's poor reputation and change how customers regard your team. The system made it hard to succeed. You've had to fire some people, including some you liked. You had to forget what you knew and do things the right way, not the easy way. You had to change how you saw your job, and there was no guarantee your strategy would work. You fought through mountains of corporate bullshit, bureaucracy, and politics and said, "Fuck you, we're going to be badass anyway, on our own terms, because we want to, and we think that's dope."

It feels good because being a Badass IT Support team is a fucking blast. Your customers love you. The only repetitive part of your job is hearing how great you are. Who gets tired of that? Instead of micromanaging and trying to get all your techs to do an awesome job, you now get compliments and respect in meetings because your team is chock-full of IT rock stars.

IT workers on the front lines of a Badass IT Support team benefit as well. You are excited about coming into work each day. You have rewarding jobs that you do well. You interact with coworkers who need you and appreciate your help. Some of those coworkers hang out in your IT area just because it's the cool place to be.

Executives love winning too. Badass IT Support gives you more leeway and budget to make cool shit happen. You can do your job without hearing how your IT guys annoy your peers and their assistants. You can build an awesome infrastructure and collect those CIO-of-the-year trophies and do interviews about how you revolutionized IT support. Plus, because you have fixed IT at the company, you get to show the CEO a beautiful QSTAC graph that's all up and to the right—proof that IT at your company is the best in the industry. Of course, you'll give all the credit to your managers and techs, but that gets you even more respect because you're so damn modest! Nice work, CIO! Here are a million stock options, you humble rascal, you. Keep up the great work!

WE WON, WHAT NOW?

The sweetest thing about building a Badass IT Support team is that you can build dope shit and think bigger than ever. This is when things get interesting.

BUILDING DOPE SHIT

At Oath, every employee has a three-word tagline to explain what they're all about. These are our personal oaths. Mine is *Build Dope Shit*. It's even on my business card. When you're badass, you can get away with a lot of things and build continually doper shit that wouldn't fly when you were a mediocre IT org.

Imagine you're the manager of a hidebound, old-school IT operation and you walk up to the CEO and announce, "Hey, CEO, we're going to build an app, some chatbots, and the conference room of the future. It's gonna be awesome. I just need two engineers and a million dollars. K? Thanks!" That CEO would laugh you out of her office and berate her assistant for letting you in.

When you run Badass IT Support and make the same proclamation, you get the budget and a fist bump for being so damn ambitious. This is when the true innovation starts. Instead of teaching social skills to your techs and dealing with disgruntled customers, you get to dream up moonshot ideas and make them happen. You can automate the shit out of all your manual processes and blow your company away with new offerings every quarter. Your CEO will be in some exclusive rooftop bar in Manhattan drinking a forty-dollar martini and bragging about you to other CEOs, who are just dumbfounded. "Wait, your IT team built a mobile app and a voice-activated conference room? My team can't even keep the printers working!"

PAYING IT FORWARD

When you're rewarded, you want to share it—especially if it can change people's lives. I've gotten pretty good at transforming IT departments into customer-centric crowd favorites. It's still gratifying for me, even though the process is predictable. I walk into a company resistant to change. I Implement the QSTAC. The IT team is skeptical. Then scores go up, the culture transforms, and no one remembers what it was like before the change.

What excites me every time is watching these IT professionals grow. Once they learn how to operate at the highest level, they get higher-paying jobs at other companies and blow their new coworkers' minds. They make six figures for the first time. Their kids get the new Air Jordans for Christmas, and their families don't stress about finances.

This is why I love what I do. I love it when people who worked for me develop the skills and knowledge to run their own teams and advance in their careers. I can't believe I get to work in IT for a living. I never imagined I'd make so much doing it. Money isn't everything, but it helps. Instead of worrying about rent, my wife and I can donate to charity, help our friends and families out, and start companies that put people first to provide careers for people who don't get many opportunities.

If more teams transform into Badass IT Support orgs,

the word will spread to other teams at other companies, and they'll get on board too. They'll become experts and make a better living. Better jobs provide braces for their kids, more presents during Christmas and Hanukkah, and more street cred for IT teams everywhere. In this way, IT workers change how they are perceived, and everyone benefits from this customer-centric revolution.

I'm not bullshitting when I say I want to pay it forward and help the young guys and girls. I want to get them jobs and invest in their careers. That's why I've started a leadership training program for technicians, and that's why I mentor two or three people at a time. I feel lucky to have a job, and I want to give other people the same support I got coming up. I went from not knowing what I wanted to do in my thirties to having a rewarding, lucrative career. I'm the luckiest guy on Earth. This is so much better than being on food stamps. I don't take my good fortune for granted.

THE MAIN TAKEAWAYS

IT is different than it used to be. Everything is plug and play, and consumers are much more comfortable with their computers. They watch TV on their phones. They play interactive online games with people on the other side of the world. Two decades ago, people were baffled by computers, but now they use them every minute of every day. The knowledge divide between a customer and a computer technician is not that great anymore. If you are in IT, you must ask yourself: "What value do I provide?"

The value you provide is the experience. So, make that experience badass! You get people back to work faster, and you help them be more productive. Your social skills are just as important as your technical skills. You talk to people. You explain how to do certain things on the computer to people who could have figured it out but turned to you for help instead.

Your job is not what it was. Your tickets don't matter anymore. It's a social game now, and if you don't get that, you waste your company's money and your customers' time. If you continue not to get it, you become a waste of a paycheck, and you might want to update your LinkedIn.

This is why companies pay me—a former therapist, failed writer, and traveling musician in Central America—to come in and tell IT managers what to do. It's not because of my technical background or my IT experience. It's because of my social intelligence. That's what matters today. It's no surprise someone with a master's degree in psychology fit in with this new age of IT. That was the gap IT needed to bridge.

All of this has been serendipitous. I got into IT because I needed a job. It just so happens that the skills I had—as a waiter, a therapist, and a student of group dynamics—were just what IT needed at the time. It was like a perfect storm. You could say I was lucky, and I'd be fine with that because I happen to believe that people make their own luck. As the great Roman philosopher Seneca once said, "Luck is what happens when preparation meets opportunity." I was prepared when my IT opportunity arrived, and I seized it.

If you get nothing else from this book, get this: Badass IT Support is a win-win-win across the board.

It's a win for the techs, who once got little respect, but now can receive their due, move up in their careers, and be on great teams that accomplish amazing things. That's way better than working in a dim room full of electronic equipment and crunching tickets all day. You're respected and empowered. People love you. You have the freedom and resources to be innovative. You're trusted. You get a seat at the adults' table.

It's a win for the company because Badass IT Support helps the bottom line. Your people become more productive. They make deadlines. Computer problems no longer hang over their heads, because they have the support they need.

And it's a major win for your customers. They used to grit their teeth and put up with IT. Now they have a voice.

When you give the customers a voice and you listen and respond to them, transformation happens. We call this book *Badass IT Support*, but the goal is a badass customer experience. That's all that matters.

CALL TO ACTION

When I got to Yahoo!, it was an old company with a lot of entrenched practices. If my team and I could transform IT at a company with such an old-school mindset, then you can do it at your company. Believe me, if you made it all the way through this book, you've got what it takes. You're a badass at heart.

The steps are simple: Give your customers a voice and listen to that voice. Be scientific about it; you can't try to guess what they want. If you need a survey, call me, and I'll set you up. Be customer-centric. Make a badass customer experience your team's top priority and unifying core value. When you do that, all your decisions make themselves.

Hire creative, energetic people. Build diverse teams. Challenge them and measure their success.

Once you alter the culture, all the changes you used to fight for become no-brainers. It's easier when everyone rows in sync. IT support by itself is not awesome, but the result—the interaction and the focus on creating a mind-blowing customer experience—is incredible. Being the best in the world at something feels amazing, and after all the work it took to get there, this victory you've achieved together is an experience no one on your team, including you, will ever forget.

Now, go forth and be badass.

ACKNOWLEDGMENTS

This book may have my name on the cover, but the stories, ideas, and inspiration in these pages belong to all the people I've worked with over the years. I didn't invent Badass IT Support. We invented it. Together. In light of that, my first word of thanks goes to each one of you who hold yourself to the highest standard of excellence every day, if for no other reason than it would be boring not to. To those who think life is too short to settle for mediocrity, who go all in and follow your hearts, you are the inspiration for this book. You are the badasses that make this world a little more beautiful.

PROPS TO THE PUBLISHING TEAM

In the twelve months it took to write this book, I bounced like a ping-pong ball back and forth across the country twelve times for work, with side trips to Italy, Iceland,

Japan, and Taiwan thrown in just for fun. Oh, and I also got married and became a director at a Fortune 500 company. I was only able to put this book out in the busiest year of my life because of my incredible publishing team. These guys rock.

Tucker Max, from a phone call in January 2016 to a dinner in Austin twelve months later, you were there for the beginning and end of the process, which meant the world to me.

Elizabeth de Cleyre, my original publisher, was my weekly source of joy, enthusiasm, and encouragement for the first half of this journey. Elizabeth promised me, often several times a day, that she would never let me put out a book that I didn't love. In true badass fashion, Elizabeth decided to follow her own dreams and moved from the company. I thought the book was fucked. No one could replace Elizabeth!

Enter Ellie Cole. When Elizabeth moved on I thought my book was destined to be mediocre or worse, but Ellie brought it home like a boss. She took over, and from day one it was smooth sailing. Writing a book is incredibly hard, but my calls with Ellie always centered me and left me refreshed and excited to make the best book we could. Her enthusiasm and support carried me through the hardest parts of this process. I hate email, but every time I got a message from Ellie, my heart lit up. Writing a book can take you to dark places, and that encouragement and positivity was priceless and transformational.

Jim Sloan, my editor, is a dream come true. He dove head first into the deep end of this project and never came up for air until we were done. If this book is any good at all, it is because of Jim. I never dreamed an editor could match and sometimes surpass my own enthusiasm for the ideas in the book, but Jim just kicked the shit out of it, day in and day out. Put simply, no one person contributed more to this book than Jim Sloan.

Michael Nagin, the absolute genius who came up with the cover art. Check out his work at michaelnagin.com.

Rob Taylor, for the awesome headshots. Check out his work at robtaylorphoto.com.

John Mannion, for working with me for over a month just on the outline.

Koalas. I don't know who you are, but I know you helped. Thanks to all the Koalas who gave their input and helped out behind the scenes.

THE ORIGINAL INNER CIRCLE

This whole idea of Badass IT Support was a collaboration of a close-knit team of outsiders and outlaws who refused to play by the rules of old-school IT. Luckily, we all found ourselves at Box at the same time. That inner circle included Ben Haines, the dopest CIO ever, and Emily Feliciano, my best bud and the only IT executive whose ridiculously high standards surpass my own. I am definitely the scrub in this group. Ben and Emily took pleasure in putting me in my place when I missed the mark, and this has been my greatest source of inspiration, innovation, and humility throughout the last four years. Oh yeah, and Dave McCluskey! Dave's liver will outlast us all, and the comic relief he brings to the group is invaluable. Working with these three has brought me more laughter, memories, and gray hair than any team ever.

THE OATH CREW

Brian McGuiness, aka "Big Mac," is often the first person I talk to every morning. Thanks for the daily morning calls and for always having some crazy-ass story to tell me from the West Coast. You're a true friend, like it or not, fucker! I couldn't do what I do without you.

Steve Norton, who, although he calls soccer "football," is somehow able to manage three continents like a total boss and still be as charming and British as ever.

James Bird, who keeps me honest every step of the way

and taught me that civilized people never drink cappuccino after noon.

All my techs on the East Coast. Thank you for putting up with my unconventional leadership style and making me look good by kicking ass at what you do day in and day out. You make me proud every day. Let's build some dope shit this year!

My management team at Oath: Israel Dejesus, Edmund Eng, and Tim Maroney. I have never been prouder of a group of IT managers. They are outrageous, courageous, passionate, hilarious, and hands down the best I've ever worked with. With those three, to quote Lee Iacocca, I was finally able to "hire smart people and get out of their way."

My Special Ops team: Martin Bieniek, Jesse Vazquez, and Sean Smith. This group of guys is smarter, more talented, and more fun than any team you're likely to meet. They're ridiculous, hilarious, a little bit crazy, and have never met a problem they couldn't conquer. The stories of their conquests are classified, but their enthusiasm and positive attitudes are legendary. They are the best of the best and the embodiment of Badass IT Support.

THE SAN FRANCISCO GUERILLA DESIGN CREW

Besides introducing me to the SF nightlife and how to

work hard, play harder, and then still show up at work the next day, these women were beyond generous with their talents in helping me choose the design direction for this project:

Donna Villacorta, my twin, the girl version of me, and so on. If there is a more beautiful, badass, generous, authentic, full-of-life person alive, I certainly haven't met her.

Biki Berry. Biki is the patron saint of creative talent in tech and advertising and the most legendary person I've ever met. She's the kind that will help you in a huge way and then convince you that you didn't need her help. Biki, you know how I feel—thanks for everything.

Rachael Zak, thanks for letting a long-haired hippie stranger crash your birthday party a decade ago on a night that started a whole new chapter of my life. I think we'd all agree (especially you, Eric!), when you meet Rachael, you just fall in love with her. It's unavoidable. Rachael is the best in like thirty different ways. Thanks for everything, Zak!

Adriana Sesana, the beautiful Brazilian with the biggest brain in town. Combine creative instinct with a photographic memory, and you have a force to be reckoned with. Adriana was always the first to give me instant feedback on everything from logos to headshots. She's larger than life and will kick your fucking ass. A true Brazilian badass, that one.

And of course, the hottest lady in SF, Michael "don't call me Mikey" Richards, thanks for being kind to a young, nerdy, confused kid fresh off the boat from Guatemala and welcoming me into your group. I may have grouped him in with the girls, but Michael is 100 percent the man.

THE LEGENDS

Kristen Cordle, a true kindred spirit who in addition to being a dear friend taught me who really runs shit in the world's hottest tech companies.

Nicole Aflague, who has inspired me since the moment I met her back in 2010. Nicole is the smartest person in any room, can herd executives around like cattle, and is one of the most remarkable women I've ever met in my life.

Dick Costolo, the best CEO, ever, period. I've worked for several legendary CEOs, but Dick stands head and shoulders above them all. I aspire every day to run my own company as well as he ran Twitter. Also, he's fucking hilarious, a definite nice-to-have in start-up land.

Maggie Utgoff, without a doubt the best boss I've ever had. Badass executive and inventor of "emotional corporate check-ins," Maggie inspires me every day to be as awesome to my directs as she was to me. One never forgets their best boss.

TEAM AWESOME

The Jawbone crew: Juilan Crovetto, Brian G., and Minh Le. Julian and Minh had the dubious honor of being my first direct reports as an IT manager (sorry guys!). In spite of that, together with Brian they set the gold standard of what I now call Badass IT Support. Every success I've had in leading teams has come from trying to re-create the magic that happened when the four of us joined forces to become the most badass IT team in history. I've come close at a few companies, but I doubt any team will ever be as good as the one we had back then. It was lightning in a bottle, and I'll never forget that run.

THE CREATIVES

Gabriel Dean. From recording my first album to producing my first short film, Dean has been at the ground floor of every creative thing I've ever done. His DNA is in everything I'll ever create.

The French Connection, for your friendship and love throughout the past decade. Much love to Pierrick Varin, Nelson Melina, Julien Chapat, Bruno Wen, Grégory

Raymond, Vincent Deffes, and Noé Varin. The most amazing group of coders, artists, musicians, and writers I've ever met.

THE FAM

Monster, Quasi, and Rebbe, for putting up with me regularly staying up all night until morning writing, rewriting, and re-rewriting. Rachel, you're the love of my life, and I love you more every single day. Dogs, sorry for ignoring you all those nights and forgetting to dish out the treats. The book's done, I promise!

Cindy Brennan, aka Mama Brennan, for moonlighting as a security guard every night after teaching all day so I could go to college.

Peck Brennan, my pops, for loving me more than any father I've ever heard of and providing for us, raising us, and always being supportive and excited for what I'm up to.

Melissa Joy Brennan, my favorite sister who would visit me from afar in SF only to find me working all night at some stupid start-up or other and caring way too much about IT. Who would care about IT that much?

Maurice, my main man who knows the struggle. I know

your humble ass won't believe me, but I look up to you, man. Thanks for rescuing me from my hermit writer life-style and reminding me that actually interacting with people once in a while is dope.

Marsha and Oscar Bronsther, for raising the love of my life and for welcoming me into their hilarious, ridiculous, and lovely family as if I were one of their own.

Aunt Judy, my sanity check as I navigate the above-mentioned new family.

Jacob Bronsther, for taking time to read the manuscript and actually liking it.

Noah Shussett, for being a true brother, helping me survive the hard times, and introducing me to the love of my life.

Maddie Blumenthal, a true friend and one of my favorite people on Earth. Miss you, Maddie Bear!

Meredith Slaughter, one of the few people who knew me both down in the dumps and up in the clouds. You'll always be family, Mere. Thanks for everything.

Jo Bellomo, for all the late-night jam sessions and for generously giving me a taste of the good-life years before I could ever afford it.

THE DEPARTED

Raed Shaar, a true badass who died way too soon but lived more life in his few years than any of us ever did.

Ellyn Bronsther, who lived a legendary life and never lost her swagger, known to say even in her eighties, "Fuck them if they can't take a joke."

Marie-Claude Huard, the wonderful, warm and talented mother of two of my favorite people on earth. It was an honor to spend time with you before you passed.

Cody Bear, a big, beautiful Bernese mountain dog that brought love to everyone he met. Rest in peace, Cody Bear.

THE REST

Finally, I'd like to thank everyone who took the time to read this book. As evidenced by the length of the acknowledgments, a lot of folks put love, time, and inspiration into making this book as awesome as possible. Your reading it today means the world to me and to us.

Sincere thanks,

BB

ABOUT THE AUTHOR

BEN BRENNAN is a former psychotherapist and a self-taught IT expert. He blended his knack for repairing computers with his deep knowledge of interpersonal communication to carve out an important new niche in IT. Brennan has consulted for some of the country's leading tech firms, including Box, Yahoo, Twitter, Jawbone, and AOL, showing them how great communication, clearly defined and measurable goals, and an irreverent sense of humor can revolutionize a company's IT department. Brennan is currently the director of IT for Oath Inc.

Made in the USA
Middletown, DE
12 December 2019